DATA SCIENCE
UNCOVERING THE REALITY

IITians uncover how Data Science is transforming
some of the world's biggest companies

Pulkit Bansal *and* Kunal Kishore, *with*
Pankaj Gupta, Srijan Saket, Neeraj Kumar

INDIA · SINGAPORE · MALAYSIA

Notion Press

Old No. 38, New No. 6
McNichols Road, Chetpet
Chennai - 600 031

First Published by Notion Press 2020
Copyright © Pulkit Bansal, Kunal Kishore, Pankaj Gupta,
Srijan Saket and Neeraj Kumar 2020
All Rights Reserved.

ISBN 978-1-64587-909-1

The interviews for this book were conducted during 2019. Brief biographies of the interviewees have been written as per their professional details at the time of the interview. Please note that the interviewees might have changed their roles or started working in some different companies since then. Also companies mentioned in this book may have changed their name, or got merged or acquired with or by some other companies since the time the interviews were conducted.

Dedicated to our Parents

Rakesh Kumar Bansal & Rashmi Bansal

Yugal Kishore & Meena Kishore

Shobh Nath Gupta & Usha Rani Gupta

Phani Bhushan Sinha & Sarita Sinha

Shyam Babu Sah & Kalpna Rani

Table of Contents

ADDITIONAL THOUGHTS

Preface

Do you want to build a career in Data Science?

Do you want to accelerate your growth in your Data Science trajectory?

Do you know how AI and ML is used in the world's most successful companies?

Do you want to learn how Data Scientists actually work, their insights and the challenges they face?

If any of these questions has ever come to your mind, then you will find this book to be immensely valuable. This book is a collection of essays covering how Data Science is done at leading companies across various industries. We have been working in Data Science team at different companies in India for some time now and have faced these questions ourselves at different points in our professional journey. Our desire to share these thoughts, through the words of the leaders in this domain, is what has culminated into us writing this book.

What Is This Book All About?

This book covers interesting insights such as:

- How Uber design incentives that keep its drivers happy and loyal.

- The secret recipe Swiggy uses to recommend food items to its users.

- Data Science models used at Goldman Sachs and WorldQuant for risk-management, and profit-making from algorithmic stock trading.

- How MakeMyTrip dynamically changes price of its listed hotels based on demand, supply and a host of other factors?

- How an Indian language social network, Sharechat, is using NLP and image processing to actively engage its 70 million + users?

Each essay is devoted to one company, and is written based on thorough interviews with senior members in the Data Science team at that company. Many of the people we have interviewed are considered among the biggest names in the field of AI and ML. To the best of our knowledge, no attempt has ever been made before to write such a book which focuses on applied large scale Data Science, especially in the Indian context.

Although we will discuss here a very technical subject, this book itself isn't very technical per se. One doesn't have to know a lot about Data Science to gain value from this book. All one needs is a desire to learn about how Data Science is being applied in today's world and its impact in the industrial domain.

During our interviews, we have made an effort to unravel each and every aspect of Data Science and machine-learning work being done at these companies. This includes understanding the company's business, their Data Science problems, the ML algorithms and solution approach, technical tools employed, the challenges faced, as well as the hiring process and the skills companies look for in potential Data Science candidates. Armed with all these details, we have written each essay by summarizing all of our understanding in a simple and accessible manner.

In addition to this, we have also covered areas like "how these leaders in Data Science think that the young candidates should train themselves for a future Data Science career?," and we got surprisingly diverse answers. It was also quite interesting for us to learn that different companies have very different cultures and philosophy of doing Data Science. Consequently, we feel that depending on one's own personality and interests, people might prefer to work in some companies more than others.

Who Is This Book Aimed at?

In recent years there has been an enormous surge of interest among college students and young professionals across the globe who want to pursue Data Science as a career. We've written this book keeping them as the primary readers in our mind. Also, this work will be equally valuable to existing Data Scientists as they can gain insights from some of the best practices using which Data Science problems are being solved outside their companies.

Additionally, people working on the business side such as Analytics Professionals and Product Managers, can benefit from this book by learning various non-technical aspects of applied Data Science. Some of these are:

- When is a business problem ready for Data Science to be applied to

- How is Data Science work structured between engineers, researchers and business owners

- How advances in Computer Vision, NLP, Recommender-Systems are creating business impact

Finally, anyone who has an interest in Data Science, and wants to learn about the state-of-the-art in the industry will find this book useful.

How This Book Can Help You?

One may ask that "With so much information available on the internet, why should I ever read this book?." It's a fair question, and we believe that though one can access tons of resources on machine-learning through the internet, unfortunately, authentic information about what really goes inside the ML teams at prominent companies is non-existent. In contrast, all the information we provide here is based on actual interviews of leading Data Scientists.

To summarize, our book meets the following major needs:

- Provide real insights into how some of the best Data Scientists work and what goes into building actual ML based products.

- Give a clear picture of the challenges faced by Data Scientists in industry, the problems they are working on, and the cutting-edge ML-solutions they are developing.

- Clear any confusion from the minds of budding Data Scientists, and help them reorient their own training and learning efforts to what is truly valuable for real world problem solving.

Knowing these details will not only put you ahead of other candidates in the job market, but it will also give you insights for a lifetime. Along with any courses or training material that you are going through in your Data Science journey, learning about how the real industry works require just a bit of an extra effort. But, we believe that this investment of time and effort will definitely make you a more impactful Data Scientist.

Being Data Scientists ourselves, we have tried our best to make sure that the contents in this book are accurate, and honest. The book can be read either in chronological manner or by jumping to any chapter directly. It is recommended that the ideas that strike you as important should be marked so that the book can be referred to in a fast fashion later on.

Feedback

We would love to hear from you. While we have tried to be as accurate as possible in furnishing information in this book, some mistakes may remain. For any suggestions, comments or errors regarding this book you can reach out to Pulkit Bansal at pbansal1940@gmail.com or +91 9686055524 and Kunal Kishore at kunalkishore.iitkgp@gmail.com or +91-8105947256.

Acknowledgements

We would like to thank a number of people, without whose contributions and encouragement, this work would not have been possible. We thank Varun Modi for initially helping the project get off the ground as well as for attending & arranging several interviews. We thank Ankit Bansal for his help by attending a couple of interviews and writing initial draft of an essay. We thank Mr. Amitabh Satyam for his guidance and help regarding the publication aspects of this book.

We thank Gaurav Mittal for proofreading several essays from a product manager's perspective which greatly simplified our presentation.

Finally, we owe a big thanks to all the companies and Data Science leaders for agreeing to participate in this project, and for giving us their precious time for interviews. Among these, we owe a special thanks to Ankit Jain, Avi Patchava, Madhu Gopinathan, Rahul Jaimini and Rajesh Bansal for going above and beyond in helping us to improve these essays.

Pulkit Bansal
Kunal Kishore
Pankaj Gupta
Srijan Saket
Neeraj Kumar
February 2020

Uber
Ankit Jain

Authors: Pulkit Bansal, Srijan Saket

About Uber:

Uber's mission is to create opportunity through movement. Uber started in 2010 to solve a simple problem: how do you get access to a ride at the touch of a button? More than 10 billion trips later, we're building products to get people closer to where they want to be. By changing how people, food, and things move through cities, Uber is a platform that opens up the world to new possibilities.

About Ankit:

Ankit currently works as a Senior Research Scientist at Uber AI Labs. He has also co-authored a book titled "Tensorflow Machine Learning Projects." Additionally, he has been a featured speaker at many of the top AI conferences and universities across the U.S. including UC Berkeley and the O'Reilly AI conference. Outside of work, he has mentored over 500 students in AI through various startups and bootcamps. He received his M.S. from UC Berkeley and BTech from IIT Bombay (India). Previously, he has worked at Bank of America, Facebook, and a few startups.

1. My Data Science Journey

I completed my undergraduate degree from IIT Bombay in Electrical Engineering. There I got my first experience in statistics and its applications by taking courses like signal processing and wireless communication. Post-graduation, I worked at Schlumberger as a Senior Field Engineer for 3 years.

Although working at rig sites was exciting, I felt that my talent and interests lay in something more quantitative. Therefore, I decided to complete my Masters in Financial Engineering at UC Berkeley. While at UC Berkeley, I pursued a Data Science internship at Facebook where I contributed to the "Pages You May Like" feature. After receiving my master's degree, I worked in bond trading at Bank of America Merrill Lynch. However, after a year of doing finance, I realized that I was missing the fun of working at a tech company. This motivated me to move back into information-technology sector. Initially, I worked for a few startups in San Francisco and India before joining Uber AI.

2. Data Science in Logistics

At a very high level, common logistics challenges across industries include:

a. Efficiency and reducing wait time

b. Improve reliability

One brute force way to achieve the two objectives is to have infinite supply in the system. In such a scenario, whenever you request the said product, you will definitely obtain one. However, such a setting is practically infeasible. One of the tools which can be used to achieve the two objectives with minimal costs is Artificial Intelligence.

3. A Glimpse into Data Science and AI Labs at Uber

At Uber, many of our teams incorporate Data Science into their technical and product-related work, including our Marketplace Team, our Rider and Driver Experience teams, our Uber Eats team, and Uber AI.

I currently work at Uber AI, the AI research arm of Uber Engineering. At Uber AI, researchers work both to advance the basic state of AI through research areas like reinforcement learning and computer vision, as well as solve AI problems pertinent to Uber's business.

Connections, on the other hand, consists of researchers who are mainly solving AI problems pertinent to Uber's business. We mainly work on solutions which can bring a step change to the existing algorithms. Some of the things our team has worked on are:

- Forecasting using deep learning to predict trips to guide budgets, pricing etc.

- Building an ML framework to deploy models at scale very easily and perform efficient hyperparameter tuning using Bayesian optimization techniques.

- Developing state-of-the-art, automated models to improve customer support at Uber.

4. Data Science Opportunities at Uber

Like most companies, a core objective at Uber is to improve user experience on the platform.

Forecasting as it relates to improving ETAs and predicting user supply and demand during high traffic events, as well as optimizing business decisions for long-term growth and sustainability across the company. Following are some of the problem types in this category:

- **Long-term Forecasting:** Uber uses forecasting to make certain business decisions. A long-term view is useful for financial planning and on-boarding new drivers.

- **Short-term Forecasting:** Anticipating supply/demand imbalances before they happen helps ensure that the Uber Marketplace remains healthy.

- **Real-time Forecasting (anomaly detection):** Having minute-by-minute forecasts of all major metrics allows us to automatically detect outages and issues on our platform.

Following are the details of some of the other major projects that are tackled with AI at Uber:

1. **ETA Estimation:** ETA estimates are very important for riders and drivers. We use machine learning for estimating the ETA's for every trip on the platform. Some of the factors that can affect ETA are (a) current traffic conditions (b) weather (c) origin and destination locations (d) past traffic conditions of the same hour & day of the week

2. **Dispatch:** Dispatch is efficient matching of drivers to riders when they request a ride. Dispatching a driver to a rider is based on a combination of factors including ETA. For carpool, it is based on percentage of route overlap between riders' routes to destination.

3. **Supply Allocation to Busy/High-Demand Locations:** Each driver sees a heat map reflecting surge amount (this is in the driver's app). Such incentive structure automatically make drivers gravitate towards higher surge locations, which in turn helps to solve the overall supply problem.

4. **Self-driving Cars:** This is one of the most challenging problems in the industry. We need to design a system that can handle uncertainty and has extremely high degree of accuracy.

5. **Other Use Cases:**

   a. **Customer support:** Help customer support agents respond to tickets via our Customer Obsession Ticket Assistant (COTA), which leverages Natural Language Processing to provide quicker and more accurate customer support ticket predictions

   b. **Fraud:** At Uber, we deal with multiple types of fraud, such as payment fraud and incentive abuse.

5. An ML Problem I Worked on at Uber: Driver Incentives

At Uber, we offer driver-partners promotions like Quest and Consecutive Trips to bring balance to the marketplace and maximize driver earnings. With consecutive trips, drivers are paid more to complete consecutive trips during busy hours.

I've worked on the problem of allocating incentives budgets for different cities and based on trip demand. Essentially, we want to distribute the global incentive budget efficiently into different cities so as to optimize user experiences for riders and driver-partners alike based on demand.

To solve this problem, we forecast driver-partner trips for a given incentive. A change in incentives can lead to different behaviour by a driver; therefore, the number of trips may vary. From machine learning standpoint, it can be framed as a forecasting problem. We use historical time series driver data of three kinds:

- **Static:** City, acquisition channel, acquired month etc.

- **Behavioral:** Trips, Supply hours, accepts, rejects, cancellations, earnings, referrals, % surge-trips etc.

- **Incentives:** Dollars earned historically through incentives, budgeted incentive data for the driver for future.

For modeling, we use a deep learning approach to forecast driver sensitivity with respect to incentives, more specifically it's an LSTM based forecasting model with "zero-inflated Poisson loss." We build a separate model for each city.

6. Skills Required for Data Science

On the technical side, one should have solid fundamentals of maths/ statistics and machine learning. Knowledge of programming is required to code up your ideas and also to deploy machine learning models into production.

Other than technical skills, you need to have curiosity for data and the ability to ask the right questions. When it comes to solving a business problem at hand using Data Science, things are never straight forward. "Why are users uninstalling the app? Why drivers are rejecting ride requests? Why are the riders not using the app over the weekend?" Questions come in plenty with no formulaic Data Science applications. Before applying any tech skills, you need the ability to map the business problems to Data Science. Once you have defined the problems in mathematical terms, technical skills come in handy to solve the problems in the most efficient manner. In conclusion, pure tech skills may help in solving only a small part of the problem. One has to apply business intuition, consider domino effects and acquire other skills if necessary, making the entire journey very challenging.

Additionally, if you are considering a research career, then the ability to read and understand research papers is quite important. Reading papers helps you understand the state of the art in the field and also advances your AI knowledge.

7. My Advice to Aspiring Data Scientists

The first thing one should do is to pick-up a language either python or R. Then you should get a basic understanding of statistics & linear algebra. With these skills now you are good to start doing projects. You can also add research paper reading component to this if you wish to learn more about the cutting edge techniques. It is good to maintain an online portfolio of projects on Github, or if you can publish your work on a blog that's even better. If you are interested in developing deep learning projects, you can read my book on **Tensorflow Machine Learning Projects** (available on Amazon) [1]

If you choose to do research, then you should focus on a single domain (e.g. Recommendation Systems, NLP or Computer Vision), because in research, depth is much more important than breadth. When you come into industry you also need a knack for business. You should be able to design the correct business-specific metrics to optimize for, based on a vague problem definition.

Writing great points on CV is very easy nowadays. In our interviews, I look for how well you can explain a project that you have done. Do you understand all its details in & out? Even if you don't do so well at coding interview it might be okay, but not knowing what you have done is not acceptable.

Also, there is a prevalent notion that acquiring machine learning skills alone will make you a Data Scientist. But in reality, to get the most out of a model you have built, you need to communicate the results of your model to stakeholders in a non-technical way. This will require you to explain the complex statistics concepts such as p-value, F1-score in layman terms. If you are in college, the best way to pick up these skills is to write a blog/presentation about your project and share it on social media. This way people can respond to your work and give you feedback on your writing as well as your technical skills.

To summarize, pure tech skills can get you into the top 10% of candidates, but after that the journey is hard and you must acquire other non-technical skills.

References

1. *TensorFlow Machine Learning Projects: Build 13 real-world projects with advanced numerical computations using the Python ecosystem,* Ankit Jain et al. https://www.amazon.in/TensorFlow-Machine-Learning-Projects-computations/dp/1789132215

2. *Using Artificial Intelligence in Logistics at Uber,* Ankit Jain https://www.slideshare.net/AnkitJain259/ai-in-logistics-at-uber-89300292

Swiggy
Kranthi Mitra, Dale Vaz and Amit Garde

Author: Kunal Kishore

About Swiggy

Swiggy is one of the leading food ordering and delivery platforms in India. It was founded in 2014 by Sriharsha Majety, Nandan Reddy and Rahul Jaimini who are graduates of BITS Pilani and IIT Kharagpur. In a short time span, it was able to achieve the unicorn status (over $1 billion market valuation). Today, Swiggy operates in more than 25 cities of India, has partnered with 55,000+ restaurants, and has over 10 million downloads of its Android and iOS apps combined together. Till date, Swiggy has successfully delivered more than a billion orders across India.

Brief Biography

Dale Vaz, is currently the head of Engineering and AI at Swiggy. Previously, he was the Director of Software Engineering at Amazon India, heading the Consumer and New Businesses. He completed his B.E. from Manipal Institute of Technology in 2000 where he was ranked 1st in Computer Science, received the Best Student Award and a Gold Medal. He also completed his MBA from the University of Massachusetts Amherst in 2007.

Dr. Kranthi Mitra Adusumilli leads Data Science Team at Swiggy currently. Previously, he was Senior Principal Data Scientist at [24]7. He completed his B. Tech degree from IIT Delhi in Production and Industrial Engineering in 2002, and then, his PhD in Operations Research from the University of Texas at Austin in 2007. He holds several US patents in areas such as intent-prediction, user-profiling and ad-word optimization.

Amit Garde is currently Vice President of Engineering at Swiggy where he is responsible for creating engineering platforms. Previously he has worked at several companies such as InMobi and Bloomreach. He completed his Master's degree from IIT Kanpur in 1993, and was a graduate student in the PhD program at IISc. Bangalore, where he worked on query processing for massive scale databases.

1. Applied Mathematical Problems at Swiggy

Swiggy's entire business can be looked at as a three-way market place, whose components are consumers, delivery executives and restaurants, and each Data Science problem is associated with one or several of these components. Applied mathematical problems at Swiggy are of two types: (1) Operations Research based and, (2) Data Science based. Another way of classifying the problems will be to break them into pre-ordering and post-ordering for the consumer. Below, we delve deeper into these problems while taking a three-way marketplace point of view.

Customer Point of View

First problem is that of restaurant recommendation, in which users need to be shown relevant restaurants. This can be done at a global level so that each user in a certain area zone is shown the same ranking of restaurants. But a better solution would be customer specific ranking of restaurants, based on the current context when he opens the app, and his tastes and food habits. Another interesting problem is what food dishes, across restaurants, to recommend to a user in the 'Swiggy Pop' section. Here different algorithms are used such as association rules (e.g.: recommend 'rajma chawal' this time because the customer has ordered 'chole chawal' multiple times previously).

Being a diverse country, India has a variety of cuisines and also, many a time, the same dish is known with different names (for e.g.: 'fish tandoori' in central India vs 'machhii tandoori' in West Bengal). Hence the first requirement is to create a country-wide exhaustive food catalog, which is itself a challenging process. This involves image to text retrieval using deep learning techniques. Then, based on what customers have ordered in the past, a user profile is built against the food catalog. This task is known as 'recipe mining' as it employs techniques from the area of data mining. Now, using this user profile and the food profile of each restaurant, a recommendation system is built which throws out a personalised rank of a restaurant against each user. In this model, other aspects like spending appetite, day of the week, preference for speedy delivery etc are also included to make the results truly satisfying for the end customer. With a few recommendation systems already in production, the team is also experimenting with advanced recommendation algorithms such as DeepFM (deep factorization machines).

Other instances of customer focussed problems are targeted discounting, i.e. different discount on different food dishes for each customer based on their past food preferences, and targeted marketing campaigns. An example of the latter will be what food dishes should be shown in the mobile ads to a mobile user, while showing the ad of Swiggy app, so that the mobile user has higher chances of installing the app.

In order to address complaints and issues raised by customers, Swiggy has developed a chat-bot which chats with customers based on drop-down list of questions and answers. They are in the process of making a more advanced chat-bot which can interact with the customers using pure Artificial Intelligence instead of taking the current rule-based approach.

Delivery Executive Point of View

The delivery fleet is responsible for handling the logistics of picking and delivering the food. They mostly care about their earnings-per-hour, and to maximize that, their wait time at the restaurant for pickup needs to be minimized. The time guarantee of delivering food to the customer has to be honored as well, in order to keep them happy. In essence, this problem has three pieces: i) time to arrive at a restaurant ii) time for restaurant to prepare the food and iii) time to deliver the food at customer's doorstep. Each of these need to be predicted in real time, so that the decision of assigning the delivery guy to the order can be done efficiently. Combinatorial optimization and mixed integer programming based 'Vehicle Routing' solutions are used here.

As the delivery executives are employees of Swiggy, some important questions to address are (1) How many executives should be employed and during what hours, so as to maintain a balance between executive's earnings and Swiggy's margins? (2) What should be the incentive mechanism to keep the delivery executives happy? Currently, the system follows an "effort based" payout and bonus system which is based on a computed value of the total effort it took for the executive to complete his delivery. Also, the delivery-fleet always have the expected payout visible to them before accepting any order-delivery.

Another interesting and challenging problem is how to batch customers' orders together. Currently small batches are operationalised. The total number of permutations and combinations of choosing the right delivery executive for the right restaurant and the right batching of food orders goes up exponentially as the batches become larger. Also, information comes into the system in real time, which makes the process of making the most optimized decisions even further tough.

Swiggy is also working on native solutions for smaller Indian cities. For example, google maps are not detailed enough to capture geographical intricacies of these areas. Hence the delivery fleet has issues in locating the correct home address to deliver the food. This results in lesser payout to the delivery executives as well as disgruntled customers. Swiggy is coming up with its own map-based solutions, to enhance the existing maps API, to overcome these constraints.

Restaurant Point of View

Supply chain and inventory optimization is needed to achieve maximum volume and margin for the restaurants. Currently, more than 55 thousand restaurants across India have tied up with Swiggy. Demand forecasting using time series techniques need to be done for popular food dishes so that they can be prepared in optimum quantities. For example: how many orders of 'Chicken Biryani' to expect from a particular restaurant on a Friday night. This is a difficult problem statement and hence a conservative approach is typically taken so that no food gets wasted. Also, this solution is applied to only select popular restaurants which need this solution the most. Other challenges are to suggest cuisine to restaurants or suggest discounts on specific dishes to increase volume or margin etc.

Another futuristic project under progress is how to standardize the quality of food under high volume scenarios. Cameras plus deep learning algorithm can be used to detect if the food is ready and thus ease the process of food making in the kitchen. Domino's Pizza Inc. has implemented a project on this line in Australia.

Swiggy Point of View

Thus the overall system is very complicated and Swiggy has to achieve maximum utility for everyone including itself. Hence it becomes a multi-objective function which needs to be solved while meeting the unit economics' constraints. There are three subcomponents of the entire end to end problem. First is the set of stochastic (or random variable) outcome prediction using supervised machine learning algorithms. These are currently done using tree-based or neural network based algorithms. Second is the area of Operations Research where, even in the presence of perfect information, an exact solution is hard to find. Hence here greedy methods or Hungarian methods are used to achieve nearly optimal solutions here. The third area to address is to deploy real-time prediction services with low latency and high throughput, as solutions are often built on top of each other, leading to dependencies.

2. The Engineering Side of Data Science at Swiggy

Swiggy received 40 billion events last year itself, and the numbers are expected to rise exponentially. To address this, Swiggy has invested heavily in building in-house data and ML platform on top of Amazon S3 cloud service. These platforms act as a horizontal in the company providing data and ML solutions across different business verticals.

'RILL' is an in-house Apache Flink based centralised data streaming platform, which helps engineers across the company to deal with real-time data consumption. Another platform they built is their central Apache Kafka service. There are many engineering teams at Swiggy which need Kafka service as a peripheral need for their core projects. Without this central service being available, they will have to build and manage their own Kafka clusters resulting in duplication of efforts. Thus this central service comes in handy in fulfilling the throughput and latency requirements of most of the engineering teams.

"Vidur" is an in-house ML platform which Swiggy team has built and this has helped its Data Science team to deploy their Machine Learning and other data-driven mathematical solutions in a robust and efficient fashion. The motivation behind building this platform is that Data Scientists are definitely the experts at building an accurate mathematical model but they lack the advanced engineering skills to deploy their model in real time or batch fashion. Vidur has several components such a data exploration, prediction service, model performance monitoring etc. This platform has reduced the gap between model development and deployment from months or weeks to a matter of days resulting in faster experimentation with models. The reason for building an in-house platform instead of using somewhat generic external tools like Amazon Sagemaker is that they wanted a customized platform that can address the specifics of Swiggy's needs.

3. Challenges in Developing In-house Engineering Platforms

There are few broad themes which come up frequently in building an engineering platform at a technology-based company. The first is how to handle the current huge scale of data and the further scale-up of data in future as the company grows exponentially. This is particularly true for Swiggy as it has witnessed massive exponential growth since it was launched in 2014. The experts have to build system components in a preemptive fashion, anticipating the worst case scenarios. Often things break at scale and the platform has to be able to handle it.

Secondly, a challenging question to answer, with little information at hand, is to what tools to use as a core part of the platform concerned. As there are multiple open source as well as paid softwares and frameworks available, it doesn't make much sense to build a platform from scratch. Rather, an efficient approach would be to leverage some of these tools and build upon them a system which caters to the pre-decided objectives. However, there are a plethora of such tools for any given task. For example, few tools which offer real-time data streaming facilities are Apache Flink, Apache Storm, Amazon Kinesis, Apache Kafka, Apache Samza etc. Each of them offers certain overlapping functionalities as well as some non-overlapping specific capabilities. One cannot take an A/B testing approach in deciding which tool to go ahead with, as the life-cycle of platform development is long and very time and effort consuming. In such a situation, leaders try to do rigorous analysis of each of the competing tools, delve into their details, talk to competitors, attend conferences, so as to gather as much information as possible. Then they do a cost-benefit analysis to decide which tool to go ahead with. Sometimes there are failures and then course correction has to be done.

Third area to focus on is how to democratize the use of the platform concerned. It is desired that certain platforms such as Machine Learning platform should be able to cater to people with or without technical expertise in it. Here it will mean that even the Business Analysts or Product Managers in the company should be able to use the platform, resulting in lesser dependency on the core Data Science team for a project to be picked up.

4. Team Structure of Data Science at Swiggy

Swiggy has a core Data Science team which has recently been divided into two parts. One is focussed on short-term problems where the life cycle of project can vary from a month to six months approximately. The second part of team is focussed on research and looking to solve challenging problems in the area of operations research, computer vision, and NLP (natural language processing) etc. with a longer time horizon.

Model deployment is primarily owned by the Data Scientist who has developed the model. At Swiggy the Data Scientists use in-house ML platforms such as Vidur for prediction service, and they build the online data and training pipelines by themselves in Scala. There are also few Machine Learning engineers who can help, if needed, in deployment and consumption of complicated Machine Learning services.

5. Pros and Cons of Having a Data Science Team in India vs Abroad

Working with a Data Science team from a native country has some very good benefits. For example in the USA, residential or commercial addresses are very systematic and easily understood whereas in India, such addresses can be a little complex to interpret. Correspondingly we need suitable solutions to detect address quality. Similarly, traffic congestion scenarios in USA and India have a stark contrast between them. Data science solutions around delivery time prediction etc will have to incorporate these differences to ensure accuracy and robustness. It is true that these intricacies can be communicated and discussed with a non-native team working outside of the country so that they can incorporate appropriate techniques. However, lots of deep-seated issues can easily get missed out due to a lack of personal experience of such native nuances. If we have a native team who understands and experiences such ecosystem constraints, then they are able to come up with more realistic and effective solutions.

A con of this situation is that Data Science teams in mature technology markets like USA or China have a higher inclination towards research as compared to that in the upcoming countries like India. The companies over there have larger budgets and wider time horizon to spend on research, along with higher availability of research talent like PhDs in STEM (science, technology, engineering, mathematics). The applied engineering and applied Data Science talent pool in India is very capable but the culture of research will take some time to mature. Thankfully, in recent years, this trend is changing with lots of PhDs from the USA coming back to India to work with top technological companies.

6. When Should a Company Pursue Data Science Solutions to Replace the Rules-Based Solutions?

Before applying a Machine Learning solution to a problem, the first question to ask is whether the problem is ready for Machine Learning solutions? Most startups start with hard-coded numbers or averages based on intuition and domain knowledge, for numerical asks. Example of such asks at Swiggy are: expected time of delivery, expected time for delivery executive to arrive at a restaurant, list of top restaurants, which delivery executive to allot an order to in a nearby area, fraud detection etc. As the business scales, data starts coming in. At this stage, good data management is imperative so that it's easily accessible and modifiable. Then comes the inflection point when this clean data can be used from existing data lakes to run mathematical models on top of it to give dynamic solutions to the numerical asks, replacing the magic hard-coded numbers. For example, Swiggy generated 40 billion events last year and the company runs multiple Operations Research and Machine Learning Solutions on top of their data.

7. Advice to Aspiring Data Scientists

Data Science is a very rigorous job which needs an eye for details. In applied Data Science domain, one needs to understand when to work out a custom solution or when to use a pre-existing solution. Having a PhD is really useful if the problem at hand is complex and needs lots of abstraction and dissection around it. Students at college should try to do internship in companies to gain a first hand experience in Data Science. Participating in competitions on platforms like Kaggle helps in gaining knowledge too.

Swiggy looks for five traits when hiring someone for the Data Science role namely outcome, execution, technology, mentoring and influencing. Each candidate is graded on these five dimensions and then decided upon. Earlier Swiggy was more focussed on coding skills for Data Science as out of box simple solutions were the need of the hour. But now that Swiggy has basic systems in place already, the next phase of improving solutions needs in-depth knowledge of mathematics, statistics and Machine Learning. Hence, now the focus is more on depth of knowledge and less on coding skills. A PhD degrees is desirable, though not a must.

8. Future of Data Science and Deep Learning at Swiggy

Traditional supervised machine learning algorithms are very relevant even in this era of deep learning. This is because they are easier to implement, debug and deploy in terms of cost and effort. However, there are other domains where deep learning is making a lot of difference. Food catalogue creation is based on image processing of the restaurants' menu, in order to extract text and other information. There are future computer vision based plans at Swiggy to check the food quality and quantity using cameras placed in the restaurant's kitchen, before sending it out for delivery to the customer.

Swiggy is currently experimenting with deep learning models in offline mode. Recently it acquired Kint.IO, a start-up at Bengaluru that applies deep learning and computer vision to object recognition in videos. Latest advanced mathematical approaches to solve Operations Research related problems are also being tried out such as genetic algorithms, swamp or colony optimization algorithms etc. They have tied up with Nvidia for artificial Intelligence related computer hardware and systems.

Future of Data Science will be heavily correlated with software engineering, and Swiggy is pushing to use machine learning in nearly every decision-making system at their company. This will need democratization of Data Science so that the software engineering teams can also make models and deploy them. This needs huge effort to train and teach Data Science to all the teams in the company. Even business leaders will need to understand the basic aspects of it.

Goldman Sachs
Abhash Anand

Authors: Kunal Kishore, Pulkit Bansal

About Goldman Sachs

Goldman Sachs is an American multinational investment bank and financial services company headquartered in New York City. Some of its major works are trading, asset management and investment management across instruments in various asset classes such as equities, interest rates, currencies, credit, and commodities. It is one of the largest investment banking enterprises in the world, and manages assets of over 1500 billion dollars. It has over 36,000 employees working in various parts of the world, and has major offices in New York City, London, Bangalore, Hong Kong and Tokyo.

Brief Biography

Abhash Anand graduated from IIT Kanpur with a dual degree of B. Tech and M. Tech in Computer Science and Engineering, in 2012. After that, he worked at Goldman Sachs in its Market Risk Modelling Quantification group which was involved in Capital and Risk Quantification. He quickly climbed up the ladder, and became Vice President in his team. Later on, in 2017, he joined a finance start-up, Credy, as its CTO to pursue his entrepreneurial interests.

1. Broad Overview of Abhash's Work at Goldman Sachs

Abhash's role at Goldman Sachs was by its nature, very quantitative. Number crunching is a key aspect here. He worked in an independent risk management team at Goldman Sachs which performed risk analysis for different types of company's investments under different types of simulated scenarios. His role involved regular internal risk assessment for the company's multiple portfolios of instruments so that the risk at hand can be kept under strict thresholds. Keeping risk under threshold is critical to minimize company's losses and also to prevent the occurence of financial catastrophes such as the financial crisis of 2008. He also worked on regulatory projects under which regulatory bodies, such as the Federal Reserve of the USA, came to the company for risk estimation of the company's investments, with strict guidelines on framework and assumptions. His results were used to manage risk of the investments by exposure balancing, portfolio diversification etc, resulting in the company being able to successfully adhere to the stringent policies laid down by the regulatory bodies.

2. Data Science and Quantitative Problems in Risk Modelling at Goldman Sachs

Abhash worked extensively on time series data during his stint at the firm. He also worked on missing data treatment in time series. He used classic techniques like Brownian Bridge to fill in the missing values and conducted back tests to validate the accuracy of the same. His job also involved projecting extreme market scenarios over six to twelve months based on historical data and corresponding assessment of the simulated PnL numbers of the portfolio. Scenarios projected used to be based on internally created framework, or provided by regulatory bodies such as the Federal Reserve, or based on historical trends.

It is worthwhile to mention here some examples of such extreme scenarios. It could be a combination of (a) all stock prices are 30% down (b) interest rates rise by 5% (c) sudden jump in credit-risk of borrowers etc. All these shocks are simultaneously applied to understand their individual as well as combined effects generated due to their interactions with each other. By analyzing the behaviour of portfolio under these assumed "market-shocks" one can better understand the kind of risks the portfolio is exposed to, and then one can actively act towards minimizing those specific risks. It is important to note that the scenarios should neither be "unreasonably extreme" nor "too soft," but they should simulate a "realistic-representation" of what an adverse market condition really looks like, such as the events that happened during the 2008–09 financial crisis.

Another kind of risk that is estimated is called "Value-at-risk" which tells us how much value of an asset may get lost in a certain duration, with some degree of certainty. This is different from "severely adverse scenario risk" explained earlier in terms of its likelihood of its occurrence. While the former usually occurs once in a decade, the latter is observed to occur more frequently, such as once every few months i.e. here the shocks are less severe.

It is to be noted that black box type of models are of little use in supervised learning problems in the financial world. This is because the results need to be backtracked to input features of the model. Only then can the risk be understood and mitigated by analysing those causal variables. Investment banks use techniques like GARCH models, Principal Component Analysis and standard Linear Regression along with other statistical methods.

Homoscedasticity refers to the important assumption of the linear regression model which means that the error terms have a constant variance. The absence of assumption is referred to as heteroskedasticity. It is a common experience that financial data suffers from heteroskedasticity and thus they don't honour the assumptions of many Machine Learning models. Abhash used to face this situation quite often in his work and he employed several mathematical techniques to transform the data into homoskedastic space.

3. Data Science and Quantitative Problems in Pricing of Derivatives*

Apart from risk modelling, derivative-pricing is another area of finance where mathematical modelling plays a major role.

To explain derivatives, we will take the example of Fly Emirates which buys oil to fuel its airplanes. Now, Emirates can lose money if oil prices increase because that would mean their fuel costs would go up. To offload this risk, Emirates may sign a contract with Goldman Sachs that gives them a choice to buy up to 1 million barrels of oil at a fixed rate of 100$ per barrel during the next 1 year. Now even if the oil price goes to 150$, as per this contract, they can still buy oil from GS at 100$. But in return for this choice/option, GS will charge a fixed cost e.g. 20$ per barrel, because now they are bearing the risk. The net outcome would be that after paying this fixed cost once, now Emirates no longer has to worry about rising oil prices. This product is called an "option," which is similar to insurance.

The main modelling-problem here is to estimate the "fair-price" for an option (e.g. 20$ in Emirates example). If a bank charges too much then nobody would buy, and if it charges too low then it may suffer huge losses in an adverse market-scenario.

Similarly, there are other use cases such as pricing of equity-options, estimating premium for "credit default swap" product based on probability of default curve, computing fixed interest rate equivalent of a floating interest rate for an "interest rate swap."

The methods used here are based on modelling the behaviour of stock or underlying interest-rate/credit-risk as a time-varying stochastic variable, whose probability distribution can often be inferred and interpolated from prices of other basic products being sold in the market. These variables are commonly assumed to follow a Brownian motion process, though nowadays several other advanced processes are also being used.

The Nobel-Prize winning "Black Scholes Model" is a pioneering work in this field, which was the first to provide a proper framework and closed form solution for pricing equity-options. Other methods used in this field include numerical techniques such as solving partial differential equations using grid-based-method, or performing thousands of monte-carlo simulations of the underlying processes to compute average payoff from the product.

4. What Are Some Non-Obvious Aspects of Building Robust and Impactful Models?

Model monitoring and regular evaluation of the model's performance is a focus area which is of supreme importance. Deviation in the distribution of input data, with time, is a common phenomenon due to the temporal nature of the world of finance. Assumptions of the model, which hold true today, may not hold true tomorrow.

The solution here is a robust mechanism of continuously tracking different aspects of the model such as distribution of the input features, error metrics of the model's output etc. Models are tuned and re-tuned, assumptions are revisited, and feature-engineering process is refreshed as and when required to maintain the quality of the output. Goldman Sachs is a strong believer of this entire model monitoring approach and has a robust mechanism to ensure it.

Also, a common observation of Abhash is that less complex models tend to live long. Whereas complex models have a smaller life along with more rigorous monitoring needed. So a simpler model which is not so costly to maintain is preferred over a complex model, which is costly to maintain.

5. Model Monitoring and Validation Setup at Goldman Sachs*

At Goldman Sachs, there is an independent team whose sole job is to do thorough "model validation," before putting any model into production. These people are also Quants with the same skill-set as the rest of the modelling teams, but just that they specialize in model-validation rather than model development. It is their responsibility to ensure that a model in production achieves the outcome it is supposed to and all the potential causes of model-failure should be made known to the stakeholders in advance.

They test model assumptions and check if the entire modelling-approach makes sense. They also provide an exhaustive list of test cases to test the implementation which cover boundary conditions, validating model inputs, comparing model outputs with intuitive ballpark estimates, putting upper & lower bounds to ensure model output is robust to unexpected bugs. Finally, they prepare a formal document of "Model Limitations and Uncertainties" for the stakeholders to keep them informed about multiple aspects such as what are the limitations of the model, possible future work, in what scenarios may the model fail or give inaccurate results, what could be the dollar impact of those failures etc.

They are the bearer of the authority to not approve a model if it doesn't satisfy their standards. Based on this feedback mechanism, the stakeholders are able to make a decision on the model's usability. Thus, in some sense, the entire responsibility of ensuring that the model behaves as expected, relies on the "model validation" team, and they are held accountable for any failures or losses that occur due to poor quality of a model.

This practice is somewhat unique to finance industry, because the potential risk of even slight inaccuracy in the models' results can lead to losses in the order of millions of dollars.

6. A peek into the Some of the Best Practices Followed by Abhash's Team at Goldman Sachs

All the tools and frameworks used by the Abhash and his team at Goldman Sachs were built in-house. Open source tools are not used because of the dicey nature of the problems at hand. Distributed data framework and techniques were often employed as there is massive data at hand.

Data Science teams sometimes follow a popular structure where models are built by one team but they are productionized by another engineering team, with regular coordination between the two. But another structure is endorsed by some companies where both the aspects of Data Science viz model building and their deployment is done by the same team. In Abhash's team, the former structure was followed. Abhash belonged to the modelling team where quantitative skills are foremost required and the engineering team are experts at machine learning model deployment. Also, there was regular collaboration between teams based out of locations across the globe, such as New York, London, Bengaluru.

7. Career and Responsibilities' Progression in This Team

Earlier, Goldman Sachs mostly preferred PhDs in these kind of roles, with the most popular fields of PhDs being physics, mathematics, statistics etc. But lately, they have been hiring meritorious freshers directly from colleges, for these roles. Abhash was one of them. In the initial years, there is a very steep learning curve. Abhash went on a learning stint around Machine Learning, Statistics, Finance, certain subjects in Mathematics like Stochastic calculus, and Probability theory. Some of these topics are taught in the Maths department at IIT Kanpur, which, if one has done already, has an added advantage.

The company helps the employees in ramping up on domain knowledge, which is crucial to have in a finance job. Soon after a person joins the company, he or she is sent to New York office for a 4–6 week program to learn more about Finance. The program consists of rigorous daily classroom teaching and assignments along with a focus on building relationships with colleagues.

Initially one has to build relatively simple models. For example, you build models similar to what has been already built by the team, and you learn from what they are "doing" i.e. you're not doing super "innovative" work in the beginning. But you're definitely "extending their work with small but new ideas." In the later years, the focus shifts to converting a business problem to a mathematical problem and then finding a solution to it. One gets more opportunity to build more complex mathematical models with time.

8. What Did Abhash Look for While Hiring for His Team

Quantitative skills and logical thinking are a must for this kind of role. For freshers with no experience yet, lots of puzzles, fundamentals of computing and statistics, linear algebra, calculus are some of the areas focussed on in the interviews. Knowledge of the financial domain is not necessary, as it can be picked after joining the company. It should be noted that coding skills are necessary but not a focus area in the interviews for this kind of role. It is expected from the employees to be able to code their mathematical models comfortably.

Abhash has a specific advice for budding Data Scientists. According to him, Data Science is an area which requires a lot of rigor and meticulousness. Attention to the last detail is a must. Whether it be understanding anomalies in the assumption, detecting outliers in the data set, model debugging by looking in every nook and corner of the evaluation design – one can be enough thorough never. Hence, Data Science aspirants and Data Scientists should give a lot of emphasis on honing this skill-set.

9. How AI and ML Is Impacting the Future of Finance

There is a major phenomenon which has happened in the last 2–3 decades in the world of retail finance, which is the availability of consumer data. Different types of financial data of the consumer such as loans, loan repayment, mortgages, transactions, investments etc. are recorded and hence available to the financial institutions. These large data sets can be processed, analysed and used in mathematical models to take more dynamic, personalised, accurate decisions in the retail finance sector.

The same is true for corporate and institutional finance sector. Data Science is deeply integrated with each and every decision taken by the financial firms. Today even social media data like that of Twitter is used in stock price prediction. Another upcoming field with the advances in the computing power of systems is the automation of model-building itself.

10. About Credy, Where Abhash Is Currently the CTO

Credy is a digital lending company focussed on disbursing small loans to salaried people. It uses past data of the customers to make decisions on different aspects of loan disbursal such as amount of loan, interest rate applicable etc. Traditional banking system is not focussed on small loans (such as loan amount less than 5 lakhs INR) due to the high costs associated with it. Credy plans to capture this market by reducing the cost per unit of loan using different types of Data Science models.

Abhash had worked extensively in different Data Science areas of Market Risk Capital Quantification at Goldman Sachs, such as model building, model deployment, converting business problem to mathematical problem solvable using engineering etc. This enriching experience came out to be very handy for Abhash at Credy. Also, his core knowledge of finance which he had gained during his stint at Goldman Sachs proved very useful here as well.

Notes

Parts of this essay related to model validation and monitoring, and problems in pricing of derivatives (marked with [*]) are based on Pulkit Bansal's personal experience working at Goldman Sachs.

Paytm
Rohan Rao

Authors: Pulkit Bansal, Neeraj Kumar

About Paytm:

Paytm is India's leading company in digital payments and online-wallet space, with over 300+ million customers using the mobile app. It pioneered the QR based mobile payments in India. With the launch of Paytm Payments Bank, it aims to bring banking and financial services to half-a-billion un-served Indians. As of January 2018, Paytm is valued at $10 billion.

Brief Biography:

Rohan is currently working as a Machine Learning Lead at Paytm. He describes himself as a 'Numbers Guy.' He is a Kaggle Grandmaster (among the Top 250 Kagglers in the world with best rank 70th). He is also a six-time National Sudoku Champion, and became the first Indian to be ranked in the top-10 in the World in 2012. He holds Post-graduate degree in Applied Statistics from IIT-Bombay. He has been a member of Mensa (high-IQ society) since 2006.

1. Data Science Problems at Paytm

At Paytm, we have various business categories, and we are working on a variety of Data Science problems

- **Personalization of the App:** We want to show suitable banners/icons to users, so that they have the most relevant content at the tip of their fingers. We use past transactions and behaviour history of users to predict & dynamically change the content. This helps in reducing churn and enhancing the customer experience and engagement, thereby benefiting our business.

- **Optimizing Offers and Services:** The goal is to reach out to customers with offers & services best suited to them. Another related task is to find the right notification channel e.g. push-notification/message/email for each individual user while keeping in mind their preferences of communication, timing and language.

We also experiment with different contents in the notification, and based on people's behaviour choose a customized-message most suitable for them.

- **Recommendation-engine for Paytm Mall:** On the e-commerce side we have a product recommendation problem, where we wish to show the most relevant products to users with a goal to increase customer engagement, transactions and total sales on Paytm Mall.

- **Determining Credit-worthiness:** In our digital credit offering through Paytm postpaid, we need to find the user's ability and willingness to pay back the lent amount. Based on transaction history, browsing behaviour, profile and payments data, we try to predict the right postpaid credit limit for each user. For this, we solely rely on our proprietary internal data instead of using external credit-scores.

- **Churn Prediction:** There are constant activities and offerings for customers who are likely to churn (i.e. stop using Paytm), since the number of active users is one of the core metrics at Paytm. There are multiple approaches to predict the customers who are most likely to churn, which requires a fair mix of business insights and data validation.

2. Broad Overview of Models Used by Data Scientists

For different problems, we use different models. These models range from Random Forest, Logistic Regression, Gradient Boosting to Neural networks and Regularized Linear models. We generally use an ensemble of two or more models to improve the final performance

In case where we don't have initial feedback data, we use cold start techniques. Such models may have higher losses/errors initially, but as we collect more feedback data the performance of model improves.

We keep updating the model parameters frequently (as we collect more data) but the modelling approach itself is not changed frequently. We consider model monitoring and validation to be an important aspect of our work. We constantly try to improve our models, because as the business evolves an old model may no longer be optimal.

3. Paytm's Approach to Building a Recommendation Engine for Paytm Mall

At Paytm Mall our catalog have upwards of 50 million unique items from over 1500 categories, and only a small fraction of these products have view or purchase history. There is a cold start problem on the user side as well, since most users don't view or purchase enough products to reliably generate recommendations with the usual user-item collaborative filtering methods. We also wanted to recommend products from diverse categories in order to prevent any one category from dominating sales, and to maintain a 'freshness' factor. [1][2]

We decomposed the recommendation problem into the following three basic parts

- **Product Pool Selection:** First for each category, we shortlist products based on transactions data, discounts data, and visibility data. Here we use a random forest model, and we also include effects such as possible increase in sales due to higher discounts. The output of this step is a set of shortlisted products with their ranks for each category.

- **Personalization of Deals Based on User History:** We use a collaborative filtering approach in this step where we construct an item-to-item similarity matrix (based on which pair of items are purchased together) using Jaccard Similarity, instead of raw counts. Even though our data is sparse, including "browsing history" in addition to "purchase history" gives us pretty decent results.

- **User Category Affinity:** Even though we achieve some level of personalization in previous step, due to data sparsity it may not tell us enough information about all the products. Therefore we've built a separate random forest model to predict user's affinity for each category. Here we use over 6000 features describing users' view and purchase history across verticals like physical goods, digital goods, travel, entertainment, bill payments etc. We pose this as a multiclass classification problem where we are trying to predict the next category where a user will make a purchase. The output of this step is the rank of each category, and percentage of total items to be picked from each category.

Later we built an improved neural-network (NN) based model to predict the user-category-affinity from last step above. We first built embeddings for each category, by training a NN in such a way that given past and previous interactions, the NN can predict the current interaction. With these embeddings, and user-specific features finally using a softmax classifier in a neural network we predict category affinities (as probabilities from the NNs last layer).

Our method gave us a 3.5x lift in click-through-rate and 2x lift in conversion-rate compared to a hand-curated and naive rule-based approach we were following earlier.

4. Project Structuring and Management

We get projects from people on the business-side at Paytm, who define the vision and roadmap of various projects. These problems are often vague and not posed directly as a Data Science problem. Therefore, the first step is to deep-dive with business-side to gain a better understanding of the problem and the constraints. The next step is to formulate it as a Data Science or optimization problem with correct evaluation metrics.

Post this step, we can start gathering relevant data and build features based on the insights we gain from the data. We then design a quick prototype model and estimate a realistic outcome from our work. This step is important, and we should make the project-manager aware of the potential upside as well as constraints/limitations of any model we are building. For example, if only 20% conversion improvement is possible with a new model, then business-people should be informed about the same in advance so that they don't have unrealistic expectations such as 50% improvement.

Once we get an initial feedback, we proceed to work rigorously on the model setup, testing, and productionisation.

5. Data Science Team Structure

The core Data Science team is spread across Toronto, Noida and Bangalore offices. FinServ team, where I work, is mostly based out of India. There is no separate Data Engineering team, as it can lead to friction and complexity. Therefore, we do the entire end-to-end productionisation as a single team. We do all the aspects of Data Science ranging from data cleaning, data storing and smoothening the access to data queries to productionizing the models. We maintain our own clusters/pipelines/serving API etc. There is a separate Data warehousing team that is responsible for maintaining and storing data.

6. Tools/Techniques/Tech-stack

At Paytm the quantum of data that we deal with is in multiple petabytes. Given such large volume, aggregating, cleaning, and sanitizing it is a big challenge. Initially 60% of our time used to go into these steps, but now this has come down to 20% due to automated centralized systems developed by our teams. Most of the data warehouses are MySql based with S3, HDFS used as data lakes.

We heavily use open-source tools like Apache Spark for our data pipelines and basic models, Tensorflow for scalable production models, Python for integrations, scheduler tools like Oozie and Azkaban for maintaining our jobs, and Jenkins for automated deployments.

7. Best Fit as a Data Scientist at Paytm

Given the complexity and variety of problems and the scale of data that we operate with, we always look for candidates with strong analytical skills and experienced engineering mindset. The candidate should be able to create visualizations, summarize and extract features at various levels of depth using a programming language such as Python or R.

The candidate should be able to delve deep into any business challenge and extract insights to ultimately build a modeling pipeline and productionize the solution. While there aren't many opportunities to work on problems at Paytm's scale, the ownership and energy of a candidate to learn and work hands-on on different components of these projects, is what would make someone perform well at Paytm.

I personally prefer to work on multiple problems at the same time, and try to do them using multiple approaches. Since, you never know what will eventually work out, I believe that acquiring this "multitasking-mindset" is necessary to succeed.

8. Advice to Budding Data Scientists

I think that beginners should put effort to learn the basic concepts of Data Science, data engineering and machine learning first, before jumping into problem-solving. Once they learn the basics, they should try to get their hands dirty onto as many Data Science problems as possible. I would also encourage people to participate in hackathons.

The approach I first took was to learn a basic set of modules/libraries, and start building simple models. Later, as I learnt about more advanced methods, I kept on improving my models. One should also learn about a diverse set of business problems, then try to formulate and solve the Data Science aspect of it.

When I started, I didn't have much background in programming and software engineering. So, I spent an entire year to improve my understanding and hands-on skills in these fields. In a similar way, one should really focus and work on improving their abilities in areas where they are weak. Learning is a continuous and rigorous process and it needs dedicated investment of time and effort.

References

1. *Recommendations at Paytm, Paytm Labs blog,* https://www.paytmlabs.com/recommendations-at-paytm/

2. *A Journey to Semi-Deep Learning at Paytm, Paytm labs blog,* https://www.paytmlabs.com/a-journey-to-semi-deep-learning-at-paytm/

Sharechat
Ayush Mittal and Irfan Hudda

Authors: Srijan Saket, Pulkit Bansal, Neeraj Kumar

About ShareChat:

ShareChat is a social network for the next billion internet users in India. It supports 14 different Indian languages, and has over 70 million monthly active users. It is a platform where users can share videos, memes, opinions, engage with celebs, and build their own follower-base. ShareChat was founded by Farid Ehsan, Bhanu Singh and Ankush Sachdeva in 2014 while they were undergraduates at IIT Kanpur. The platform has raised $124 million in funding since its inception. The company aims is to register 100 million users by the end of 2019.

Brief Biography:

Ayush works as a Lead Data Scientist at Sharechat. He graduated with a B.Tech. and M.Tech. dual degree in Computer Science from IIT Kanpur in 2016. He did his thesis on "asymmetric domain adaptation" in Computer Vision and NLP. He also works as a Data Science consultant and has experience working on problems across varied domains such as FinTech, Pharma, Healthcare, Manufacturing and E-Commerce.

Irfan works as an engineering lead for the Data Science team. He has done his B.Tech. in Computer Science from IIT Kanpur. He worked at VISA, India for about a year before joining ShareChat, and before that he did an internship at AlphaGrep in high-frequency trading. He was involved in open source as a maintainer for Firefox dev tools for short time. He has also contributed to rust programming language, angular, and tslint.

1. What Is Sharechat?

ShareChat started in Dec. 2014 with a simple idea of providing fresh and relevant content to users in their own language which they can forward to Whatsapp. Over time the founders realized that the tastes/likes/dislikes of Indian language users are very different from the content typically available on traditional social networks like Facebook. Looking to seize the tremendous market opportunity of the vernacular internet users of India, the founders decided to transform their idea into a full-fledged social network targeted to the particular needs of these users.

On Sharechat, the users can consume content from different categories and over 100 sub-categories such as good-wishes, shayari, politics, devotional songs, health-tips, fashion, khana-khazana, funny quotes, cricket etc. Such a unique collection of content, organized in an easily accessible manner, is what has allowed ShareChat to differentiate itself from the other established platforms.

Below are some fascinating facts that throw light on why Sharechat has been able to rise at such a rapid pace, and will likely continue to grow in the Indian language content landscape

- India has 30 languages with more than 1,600 dialects.

- Indian language internet users have grown from 40 million to 230 million during 2011–2016. They are expected to cross 500 million by 2021.

- There are over 200 million Indian language internet users compared to 175 million English internet users.

Source: *KPMG, Google.*

2. Data Science Problems at ShareChat

- **Personalized News Feed:** The biggest Data Science problem, which is in fact a union of many smaller problems, that we are trying to solve at Sharechat is to show relevant content to each user. The feed shown on the app should truly capture user's interests, while at the same time make him explore new things. We have to make sure that our algorithm maintains a clever balance between exploration and exploitation. In order to solve this problem, we take all kinds of historical data of the post and user into account. We see what kind of posts, tags or categories has the user been engaging with on the app. The user sees popular as well as new posts in his feed which are selected using the algorithms to suit his personal taste.

- **Cold Start:** If you have historical data for a user it is relatively easy to recommend content to him. But, what content to show to a user when he signs up for the first time on the platform is a non-trivial and significant problem for us. It's especially challenging due to the enormous variation in the likes/dislikes of users across the country.

- **Filtering Adult Content:** On Sharechat we have strict guidelines that users adhere to. We do not allow any malcontent including pornographic, violent, spam and other posts where there might be an issue of consent on Sharechat. In case a user is caught indulging in such activity, appropriate action is taken against him, and repeat offenders are blocked. Many pre-trained models that exist online don't work well enough for our setting because their training dataset doesn't contain enough Indian images. We therefore, ensure that our models are trained on the data that comes to Sharechat. This enables us to detect offensive content more accurately. We have developed a content moderation pipeline which generates metrics such as probability of a post being offensive, user history, the tag used while creating the post, presence of adult words etc. All these features are clubbed together to flag the posts which might be violating the content policy.

- **Generating Metadata:** One of the unique challenges we face is the lack of metadata. For e.g. a chair on Flipkart would have information like color, dimension, material etc. whereas for a new post on ShareChat we have almost no metadata. A major problem for us is to correctly categorize a post as user's tags could be unreliable or may not be accurate enough for our platform. For instance, a user may post a tag such as "#MyFavPic," and it could actually be a picture of Indian Cricket Team winning the world cup. This post should ideally be visible to people interested in "Cricket" category, and "World Cup" sub-category. But since we didn't get any such information directly, the only way for us is to use techniques such as label detection in images, and optical character recognition to understand the content of a post. In addition to this we use user tags, adult label, type of post etc. to generate "static meta." We also generate "dynamic meta" based on the response of other users towards a post. The ensemble of these two sources gives us a representation of a post.

- **Finding Duplicate Images/Videos:** There are many cases when people download an image or a video and post it again from their account. Sometimes it may happen that such a post becomes more popular than the original content. This may discourage the original creator of the post. Hence, it's essential to give credit to the original creator. We are using deep layered CNNs in order to find duplicates. We believe that if we start rewarding the original creators, then people will be automatically motivated to share new content.

- **Other Problems:** In addition to the above, we work on many other problems such as flagging users who post bad content regularly, targeting new customers, finding new variables that might contribute in developing and testing the algorithms, analysis of the users who leave the platform etc.

3. Sharechat's Approach to Generating Personalized News Feed

As mentioned above, personalizing the news feed to improve user-experience is our biggest and most important problem. The challenge is to ensure that out of 1 million + posts created daily on the platform, only the most relevant content is shown to the user. In our approach, we divide this task into several sub-problems and the details are as follows:

- The first thing is to analyze the behaviour of a user on the platform. What kind of posts is he engaging with, what are the genres/ categories he is interested in, how often does he engage with the creator of a post, are some major factors we consider while computing the relevance of a post for a user. This captures the part where we "exploit" on user's history to show him content he will most probably find relevant. We also ensure that the posts which have already been seen by a user don't show up in the feed.

- Alongside exploiting the user history, we also want to make sure that a user is able to explore different kinds of posts available on the app by suggesting him suitable posts. Our algorithm gives ample opportunity and visibility to a new post to rise in popularity. This poses a challenge as new content also needs to be sent to the right users. We circumvent this issue by selecting users who have high affinity towards such posts, which is computed based on the user's history and post's metadata. In summary, a user sees a mix of popular as well as new posts in his feed, and we try to maintain a clever balance between the two.

- A major chunk of a user's feed is comprised of recommendations which are shown when a user clicks on a post to see similar posts. In order to get similar posts, we see the tag of a post, creator of a post, type of post etc. A lot of content consumption on our platform happens through these recommendations. If a user clicks on a specific tag, we show him a list of similar tags which are created using clustering techniques.

- We also suggest popular profiles that a user can follow based on his actions on the app and the profiles he follows. This way we help the user in developing his own social network which in turn is reflected in the time spent by the user on the app.

4. Role of a Data Scientist at ShareChat

A Data Scientist at ShareChat is expected to be able to handle the entire process, right from fetching the raw data for analysis to the way the final model is being incorporated in the app. He looks if the correct data is being stored in the correct form, conducts exploratory analysis to detect inconsistencies in the data, builds models with the data, analyses the performance of the models and finally deploys it on scale. The Data Science team works closely with the product managers to constantly develop new algorithms and features in order to improve the user's experience on the app.

Along with working on the algorithms, one key role of the Data Science team is to come up with new metrics that can be used to improve user experience. For example we don't have a system for direct negative feedback on our app, but we try to capture it by looking at different indicators such as time spent on the post, unfollowing a user etc. We do online and offline testing to measure the effect of algorithms we deploy on the app. A Data Scientist at ShareChat takes complete ownership of his work. It's his job to monitor all the projects he is a part of. He has to ensure that all the jobs are running smoothly, and are not consuming too many unnecessary resources.

5. Tech-Stack and Tools Used at Sharechat

Most of our data is stored on AWS databases and Google's BigQuery. We use Amazon DynamoDB to store and process all the data needed by the

APIs in the backend whereas BigQuery is used to analyze data which can be of the order of billions. The environment used is a mix of Python, Tensor flow, Pyspark etc. depending on the use case.

A Data Scientist at this firm is free to use any language he is comfortable with but the team mostly uses Python and Node.js for all the analytical and API related things. Apart from these, we use AWS services like SQS which is a distributed message queuing service, Kinesis for processing huge volumes of data in real time, Amazon ElastiCache which is a fully managed in-memory data store and cache service, and several other products. With rapidly increasing user base and massive pressure on our infrastructure, people here are encouraged to explore new tools which may be a better alternative to the resources we are using currently.

6. Challenges at ShareChat

This world of new internet users that we operate in, is very tricky. Many of our users are not experienced enough to handle a social media app. It took them some time to get used to the whole idea of a social media app. Earlier the user had to choose a tag from a set of tags while creating a post. This way we could teach them how to use tags and it has also helped us with manual tagging from the creator itself. Our app is very rich in color because our users remember the features by the color and the way they are placed on the screen. These are some of the ways in which we trained them to use Sharechat initially. We continue to educate them regarding the new features that are launched regularly, through short videos explaining how to use them. This way they can make the most of the app and we can enrich their experience on the platform.

There are several aspects that increase the difficulty of Data Science problems in our industry. Firstly, there is a high amount of variance in our dataset due to varied preferences of people across different regions. Many of the Data Science problems that we formulate as classification problems are highly imbalanced in class. Then the data that we work with is very sparse. It may be the case that a user has viewed only 20 posts out of a million odd posts that come on the platform daily. We don't have any information about all the remaining posts which the user has not seen. Due to these reasons many of the standard algorithms, applied off the shelf, don't give good results in our case.

We also face significant data engineering challenges, among which ranking posts in real time is a major one. More than a million posts are created daily on the platform. We have to rank each of these posts in order to get a relative sense of understanding about the popularity of the post on our platform. Although we don't get any immediate feedback, we still need to rank a post for all users as soon as it gets created. We also need to constantly update the scores of the posts so that we always show the most up-to-date content in user's feed.

NLP for Indian languages is still in a developing stage. Some common problems that we face in the vernacular domain can be attributed to India's cultural diversity. There is also dialect change in a language like Hindi across different regions of India. On top of that many people in India tend to use Hindi and English together. Due to these reasons, we have not been able to use the full power of NLP for Indian languages. Overcoming these challenges can help us in several ways like (1) better analyze what people are writing in comments (2) gain more precise understanding of the text contained in images which will enable us to better predict the label or intent of a post.

7. Interview Process for Data Science Team at Sharechat

We encourage all kinds of applications, without putting any bars on colleges or degrees. Most importantly we look for candidates who are passionate about learning and working in a startup. It's also very important that the candidate's vision is aligned with the vision of the company. In our interviews, we like to throw new and unconventional problems at people to test how they react and deal with such situations.

More specifically, below is our interview process:

- **Algorithm and Coding Round:** The first round is focussed on concepts around algorithms and their implementations. The candidate can be asked about data structures, combinatorics or a simple question like detecting the presence of a loop in a linked list. Often the candidates are asked to code the algorithm in any language they are comfortable in.

- **Data Science problems:** The candidate is tested on standard ML algorithms and how they are applied in the Data Science domain.

The candidate is also expected to have basic skills in analyzing an experiment, AB-testing, hypothesis testing, checking the significance of a test etc.

- **Design questions:** The candidates may be asked hypothetical questions to test his /her thought process and ability to come up with new ideas. Through this process, we also want the check general problem-solving skills of the candidate.

8. Who Is an Ideal Data Scientist?

We believe that a good Data Scientist needs to be strong at data structures and algorithms. In addition, since Data Science is an ever-growing field, the curiosity to learn new things is a must. Puzzle solving also helps in developing one's aptitude for challenging problems.

The ability to formulate a problem while keeping the domain in mind is a very important skill. Once this is done, it's much easier to go ahead with choosing the right algorithm and implementing it. Domain knowledge also helps a lot in understanding/designing the features in a better manner, which gives deeper insights into the way a model is making predictions.

Although there is no general formula that can solve every Data Science problem. However, we believe that keeping the following points in mind can be very useful:

1. Identify the problem and what are the metrics you are trying to improve.

2. Formulate the problem by understanding the paradigm the problem falls in i.e. whether it is classification, regression, mix of both or something else.

3. Analyze the results of the applied method or algorithm, and then see where things are going wrong; Use this feedback to improve the performance of the model.

Regarding the qualities missing in the upcoming Data Scientists, we feel that many candidates lack the ability of formulating a given question as a Data Science problem. Moreover, many a time it happens that the candidates don't know the basics of an algorithm they claim to have applied themselves (e.g. Where does the randomness come from, in a random forest?). This restricts the vision of the person working on the problem in context of the algorithm. So people should have a basic understanding of how the algorithm works rather than just looking at the results. On using multi-layered neural networks, we feel that though Deep Learning is a very powerful tool, but it should not be used everywhere without thinking. People should learn when to use what techniques and the pros and cons that come with them. For e.g. Let's say, we want to know the reasons because of which users churn out. Here something like an *autoencoder* won't work because we will lose the interpretability of the original variables. Also sometimes handcrafted features, which come from understanding the problem in detail, might give fantastic results.

The candidates we come across can be classified into three broad categories:

1. Have done a few relevant courses and know how to apply the ML libraries.

2. Know the algorithms but lack the quality of formulating the problem properly.

3. Have a balance of domain knowledge and technical skills. These people know how to formulate the problem and use basic concepts or algorithms to solve them.

We feel that the third category mentioned above is the skill set each Data Science aspirant should aim to develop. Technical skills are very important but without the domain knowledge, there are high chances of losing the direction. For a new candidate who doesn't have much knowledge about the domain, it's important to spend some time in understanding the problem in order to understand the key metrics that drive the industry/ product.

InMobi

Avi Patchava

Authors: Pulkit Bansal, Neeraj Kumar

About InMobi:

InMobi provides a global platform for marketers, which enables brands, advertisers and publishers to engage consumers through mobile advertising. The company was founded in 2007 by Naveen Tewari and three other co-founders, and has a valuation of over $1 billion. InMobi has 22 offices in 12 countries across 5 continents and employs over 1000 people. In 2018, InMobi was named as one of The World's Most Innovative Companies in Fast Company's annual list. InMobi was also amongst the "50 Disruptive companies 2013" list by MIT Technology Review.

Brief Biography:

Avi is presently the Vice President of Data Science & Machine Learning at InMobi in Bangalore. Previously he worked with McKinsey and Company as a Senior Engagement Manager and Advanced Analytics Expert in London and Mumbai. He has also been the Chairman of the Management Committee of London based "Harrow Entrepreneurs and Investors Club" having 400+ members. Outside work, he has volunteered as a Teacher/Consultant with educational organizations in Nepal, China and India. Avi graduated from the University of Oxford with M.A. (Hons) in Philosophy, Politics, and Economics in 2006. He has also done M.Sc. Philosophy and M.Sc. Economics (Research) from LSE in London.

1. InMobi's Business Model

The worldwide advertising business accounts for up to $1 trillion of spends annually out of the world economy of nearly $80 trillion (Annual GDP). Advertising is done in two ways: (a) conventional or traditional (approx. 60–70% of the total) e.g. TV, print, hoardings and (b) digital (approx. 30–40% of the total and growing) e.g. web, mobile, TV programmatic, digital billboards.

InMobi's primary focus is mobile-advertising. In the advertising world, there are two main parties (a) Publishers (supply) where an ad is displayed e.g. Times of India app, or Facebook app (b) Advertisers (demand) i.e. those who want to show their advertisements e.g. Coca-Cola, Udacity, L'Oreal. Publishers – who are technology giants such as Google, Facebook, Twitter – manage the advertisements on their platforms by themselves – they act as the 'market-makers' as well as publishers. But there are others e.g. news, finance, gaming and entertainment apps, who need someone to handle the advertising marketplace for them, and this is where InMobi comes into play.

InMobi is a unique advertising network in how it maintains relationships, as well as helps in meeting the objectives for both demand and supply side. Publishers charge the advertiser on a "per-impression basis" (i.e. for every person who sees the ad). They would like to charge as high as possible, as long as some basic constraints are met e.g. don't show gambling/alcohol ads to my users. On the other hand, advertisers have a different goal which is typically to maximize clicks/purchases/app-installs per dollar spent. Clearly, both the parties are opposed, and InMobi plays the role of the "market-maker" i.e. efficiently matching advertisers and publishers. InMobi is one of the few major companies which is good at dealing with both sides of the market, as most other players are focused only on one side of the market – either demand or supply.

InMobi's main goal is to efficiently manage "ad-requests" throughout the day. An "ad-request" is a request from a publisher to show an ad, e.g. "who wants to show an ad on New York Times to an Indian male, aged between 18 to 21." Then an auction happens where various advertisers compete with their bids. Finally, the auction-winner gets to display its ad on the publisher's site. At InMobi, much of the process is algorithmically driven, and ad-requests typically need to be responded to within 100 milliseconds. Several billion ad-requests hit the InMobi servers every day. In a nutshell, the scale of operation boils down to around a million queries per minute. It is probably fair to say that other than digital advertising, only the very mature financial trading industry operates at this scale and speed.

InMobi is quite special in the sense that it is an Indian B2B company, which builds products, export its services (earns the majority of revenue from outside of India), and is also a unicorn (i.e. over $1 billion valuation). You would be very hard pressed to find another Indian company that meets these criteria.

One interesting question you may ask is "how an Indian company managed to do this?" I would say it is primarily because these four very bright entrepreneurs came together and made it happen, otherwise there is no special reason for this company to have come out of India in the last decade.

Our revenue comes across the world and especially the USA, China, South-East Asia and India. With over 1000 employees, ~70% are based in India itself and large teams are also present in China and the USA.

2. Data Science Projects at InMobi

Anti Fraud

A click/impression is useful for an advertiser only if it comes from an "actual person." But some fraudsters, have built bot-farms where thousands of devices are randomly clicking on the screen and generating revenues for the publisher. It is very important for InMobi's credibility to prevent this from happening. In order to eliminate these false signals from bots, we do a lot of "anomaly detection," and a combination of supervised and unsupervised learning. The definition of "what is fraud" is always changing as our adversaries are constantly developing newer methods to fool the learning algorithm. The challenge is to "pre-emptively" prevent a fraud i.e. without seeing that kind of fraud in the past data, which is not possible with supervised learning as you can only learn patterns from previous frauds. One of the areas that we are working on is how to use Generative adversarial networks (GANs) based architectures to learn and detect new and unseen fraudulent patterns. This is an exciting area of innovation.

Images (Creatives)

The goal is to answer questions such as: understand why some images work, how to optimize an image (color, size, content) to maximize its impact for each user-category, where to position the "call-to-action" button, whether to show a video or static-image? For models used here, interpretability becomes quite important as we want to understand things like "what drove the click from the user" etc. Here we are breaking new ground in how we combine the strengths of CNNs (for prediction) and Regressions (for interpretability). Generating optimal images by machine is another area that we put our efforts in.

Market Place

The advertising world is like a "market" where the price of showing ad keeps changing with time and many other factors. For example, let's say if at night people are more likely to do a click/download then there would be greater demand to show ads at night, and consequently prices would be higher at night. By making better predictions about where the market will go, we can take better actions. E.g. if an advertiser has a fixed advertising budget of $10,000 a day with which he wants to maximize his app-installs, then our predictions can help us in optimally allocating this money throughout the day with different publishers to meet the advertiser's objective. Here we have used hierarchical time series prediction models and matching algorithms. The models are built leveraging the concepts of LSTMs, ARIMAs, as well as Tree-based methods.

Behaviour Prediction

Here we work on problems like how many transactions can we expect, estimation of long-term value of a customer, and lead-generation. We have built predictive models based on a combination of Neural networks and Field-aware Factorisation Machines to enhance the click-through rate or Conversion Rate. These models are good for high-dimensional sparse feature sets of categorical variables.

Marketing Use Cases

We have built a product called PULSE for market research, where we make users fill a quick survey instead of watching an ad. For e.g. on YouTube you may have to answer a survey question with 3 options before watching a video, or sometimes in a gaming app you have to fill in a survey first before you can go to the next stage. These surveys could be useful in behaviour analysis and targeting e.g. a company might want to understand 50 year old women if they like their product-packaging, or what do guys in urban India think about a product. Here quality-detection is important, i.e. whether it is a serious response or a random one. We use tree-based methods here, with several signals such as gyro signals, user-behaviour while filling survey, and where your impressions are made on the screen. It is important for the Pulse market research product to provide the most authentic data to our advertisers.

Recommendation

The Glance app (available on Android devices) is an emerging exciting product at InMobi, where we are working to deliver content on the lock-screen of users' smartphones. In India, many Samsung and Xiaomi devices come with this product pre-installed. We want to build a recommendation engine for this to make the content more engaging for users. We are trying a combination of field-aware factorization machine and deep learning to achieve this. We really wish to take advantage of the recent advances deep learning has brought in building recommendation systems.

Supply-side Problems

We aim to show the most relevant advertisements on a publisher's page to improve their click-through rate. We have to use algorithms to learn how different page content is suitable for different advertiser demand.

Reinforcement Learning

In our case, the decisions we make in week 1, affect what will happen in week 5 or 6. We want to make better decisions about where to invest, where to explore etc. We believe that a deep reinforcement learning agent can do much better in areas of fraud-detection and marketplace prediction. This is a high priority area for us, and we want to do this at scale.

3. Tech Stack and Tools

Currently, we work on our own data centres, but we are gradually moving to cloud computing platforms. We are also increasing our GPU capacity to do more and more Deep Learning. We have distributed data framework like MapReduce and Spark to handle data at scale. For small-data modelling we use python, and spark/scala/pyspark for big-data. At InMobi, every Data Scientist needs to master these tools: HDFS, pig, hive, spark and TensorFlow for Deep Learning.

4. Culture of Data Science at InMobi

In our Data Science team, it is fair to say there is no single person who is an expert at everything, but within the team of 25, for any given task, we can find people who have real experience in the area. It is a mixture of different expertise of areas that gives the team its shape. Additionally, last year at InMobi we trained nearly 150 engineers in Data Science and machine learning. The Data Science team ran a 12-week course on Machine Learning internally. Over 100 engineers at InMobi are capable of building ML models now.

We work with a approach where a Data Scientist is pushing himself to learn and build some advanced model such as NFFM, and also mentoring 2–3 engineers for simple/low-hanging fruits on the side. If engineers know more about ML then implementation moves much faster and models can iterate faster once in production.

In my view, a Data Science solution has three major components (a) Product-based thinking to drive what problems to target with Data Science (b) The actual Data Science and modelling (c) The engineering and deployment to get the solution to impact. Data-science owns a solution end-to-end, which means that the job is not done with just building the model in part-b. It is only when you deliver final revenue impact then you 'get marks' as a Data Scientist. You will get zero recognition if you just build a model, and say "Now it's not my problem and I'll leave it to engineering to make it happen."

It is important to note that we need to finally achieve real dollar-impact for our business through our work. In our team, everyone knows the dollar-impact of the work they did this year. We encourage our Data Scientists to know the size of the pie, and estimate in advance before solving a problem what kind of impact is possible. E.g. while building an LGBM for anti-fraud, we back calculated that we need to improve accuracy by 3 percentage points to get a significant figure of $-impact per day. Without this, it would not make sense to implement the project. Our Data Scientist knew that he needed to get there, and finally after three weeks of effort he managed to get the model performance to the right level for the model to go into production.

5. Advice for Data Scientists, Skill Sets Needed to Succeed in Data Science

People can come from any background into Data Science. In my opinion, Data Science is more about having a set of intrinsic skills, though you also need to learn the hard skills to be effective. I think that Data Science is mainly about two things (a) how you think about problems i.e. asking questions such as what is the story, what is the underlying data structure, what is my objective and how to build a solution? and (b) How you get to final business impact with your solution.

I think one should build a strong foundation: invest in learning maths, and understand the core concepts and techniques behind statistics and machine learning. The fundamental structure is the same for any learning algorithm i.e. hypothesis function, cost function, and a training-technique for optimisation. Without understanding these components, you will never fully understand an algorithm. For example, we often ask during interviews about the cost function of a logistic regression, or how does the training algorithm work for logistic regression, and 80% of candidates are unable to answer that despite having applied a logistic regression in their work. I do believe it is very vital to have a comprehensive understanding of at least all the "shallow-algorithms" (i.e. other than neural networks) before progressing to deep learning. And of course you also have to code, and always be ready to pick-up new languages and tools. All of these hard skills are absolutely learnable, if you put your mind to it and have perseverance.

So, you definitely need hard skills to succeed as a Data Scientist, and everyone will tell you that. But people often don't get this advice: that this field is not just about "executing-code," and Data Scientists are actually more of "impact-scientists" – they should not forget the "soft-skills" needed for their impact. The difference between 1x and 10x impact, is often the soft-skills. Getting to impact is tough, because there are many things that can go wrong. One should be willing to get practical in your problem-solving, and persevere through issues that prevent you from getting a solution implemented, whether with people, process or the problem context.

In real-life you have to work with business, engineering, product, who are of different personalities, and build relationships with them to get the job done. This ability to build good working relationships with other people who think differently is an important skill. College is a good time to build that skill. If you do "real projects" at college, i.e. not a Kaggle competition but do something that has to change the world, whether it involves Data Science or not, you'll find how difficult it really is. When you do it, then you learn how so many forces and things get in the way to not make it happen. One needs to learn all of that through experience, and realize that success in Data Science is not just about how good you are at theory and at coding.

I think perseverance – which some people also call as grit or tenacity – makes a big difference in one's career. College is the time when you should put yourself in hard situations, and make yourself fight through to achieve something. Convincing other people and overcoming practical difficulties are big challenges, and unless you proactively do all of that you won't get to the final impact even if you have the world's best model. Eventually, your fulfilment will come only from seeing impact from your work.

Some people give reasons such as 'this is not my personality, and I'm too introvert or shy to do these things.' But I think these are excuses, and I know a number of people who are very shy or introverted but highly impactful. They have found a particular style to get to impact and made it work for them.

Another factor I believe in is that brainstorming in small groups of Data Scientists actively engaging their minds, is highly effective. For example, three of us once sat in a room and discussed about a problem related to finding whether an ad-request is coming from a commercial or residential location. We broke down the problem, and made four decisions down to what distance metric we should choose. For e.g. we estimated that Euclidean will work because of such-and-such reason. These decisions finally cracked the problem for us. This is how I think of real Data Science – the solution being fit for the problem. I definitely do not just see it as executing code.

6. How You Keep Yourself Updated in This Fast Changing Field?

Firstly one should come into this field only if they have a passion for learning. But if learning is stress, or you have to motivate yourself to learn then this may not be the right field for you, because this field is likely to only accelerate for the next 20–50 years. I keep reading 3 to 4 new papers as a weekly personal goal either in my own area or other. I do it because each time I learn something new. It makes me think about the world a bit differently. Conferences are also good but one should pick the right ones and go talk to people when present at a conference. The goal should be to learn and gain something out of it rather than sitting passively.

If you ask whether I am on top of all of the areas of Data Science, I would answer no, not at all. But the more important thing is that even if you are not the world's expert in an area, how can you make your knowledge apply to a given problem. Another thing is knowledge sharing with others. For example, I've sat and spoken in detail with people in my team who work on NLP. This has taught me at least the basics of the field as well as some important insights. Therefore whenever I might work on an NLP problem in the future, I will not be starting at zero. As a team at InMobi, we also send papers around to each other, and we have a library of over 100 good papers we have collected in 2018.

7. How was Your Previous Experience in Consulting World Different From InMobi?

When I was at McKinsey we were doing roughly one new problem/project every month. One of the things I learnt from consulting is how you take a totally new problem and design a solution from scratch. Another important part was to see firsthand that it is multiple pieces that combine together to get the final impact. Consulting makes you better at thinking about the problem, as well as you get better at dealing with, influencing and communicating with your key stakeholders, such as product managers and business leaders.

One big difference at InMobi is that it is truly a 'big data world,' and in my previous work, I never got a chance to work with such massive datasets. Here sometimes you've to do 10 joins in a query, and how you organize those joins determines whether it will take days or weeks to get the data frame right. I also learned a bit more about engineering aspects for complex solutions, e.g. latency of your model outputs; ensuring zero bugs in data processing pipelines; and how to really get the model deployed finally into production – all the steps that are needed including thinking and planning for infrastructure requirements.

8. What are Some of the Successes and Challenges Data Science Team at InMobi has Seen?

During the last one year, our team has had a lot of "zero to one" successes. Several products were launched with Data Science at the core. For e.g. we launched SmartBlocker™ algorithm as we call it for our Fraud-defence solution at InMobi. We also launched a totally new algorithm for "image and behavioural analysis" For e.g. what drives the click behaviour. Also, the marketing-research product Pulse, was newly launched with our team's work as central to determining 'authenticity' of a survey response – an innovative approach we have now filed a patent for.

We also achieved significant improvements using more sophisticated techniques. E.g. using hierarchical time-series models and LSTMs for Inmobi marketplace management, we are able to generate thousands of dollars.

We're trying to build a full end to end ML platform, and it is quite a challenge especially with different business areas having different tech-stacks. Another thing we want to do is launch a deep-learning algorithm in an online setting with 100k queries-per-second throughput, which quite possibly nobody other than Google or Facebook has done till now.

9. Future of InMobi/Advertising

We're looking forward to a future where TV will become programmatic, and video content will become highly interactive instead of passive. Movies are slowly becoming like a movie + game where a user takes actions, and based on that the outcome of the movie is determined (this is happening already with some Netflix innovations). How advertising will work in such a case still needs to be figured out. It might be that ads are dynamically placed in content based on user decisions during interactive active content, e.g. put coca-cola bottle somewhere in the scene for some users but Horlicks for others.

As an aside, the video-apps and video market is taking off really fast, and China is leading the world. For example the Chinese company ByteDance, which is one of the world's most valuable privately owned companies, owns many apps that are based on video content. These are video-first companies that have deployed Data Science and machine learning effectively, to achieve multi-billion dollar valuations.

Currently, TV operates in the same way with the same advertisements for everyone, but "Programmatic-TV" is quickly entering the market in the US. Here users will see different ads depending on their behaviour and tastes. Google is also entering into the TV market for this very reason i.e. the opportunity for programmatic advertising. Netflix is also likely to get into this space in a major way.

GE Research (Healthcare)
Chitresh Bhushan

Authors: Kunal Kishore, Ankit Bansal

About the Company

GE Healthcare, a subsidiary of General Electric, is an American company primarily involved in the manufacturing and distribution of equipment and procedures used for medical imaging such as MRI, CT Scan machines etc., besides working on different areas of health technology like IT, monitoring systems, and drug discovery. In addition, it partners with healthcare leaders, striving to leverage the global policy changes necessary to implement a successful shift to sustainable healthcare systems. GE Healthcare has over 54,000 employees located around the globe.

Brief Biography

Chitresh currently works with the GE's Global Research group as a Research Scientist in the AI and computer vision team. He completed his PhD with a focus on MRI brain image analysis at the University of Southern California (USC) in 2016, and before that, graduated with a B. Tech and M. Tech Dual Degree in Electronics and Electrical Communication Engineering from IIT Kharagpur in 2010. While at IIT Kharagpur, he also interned at CSIRO, Australia where he worked on LIDAR data reduction problems in robotics so that robots are able to effectively map and navigate through mines in Australia. During his PhD, Chitresh was awarded the USC Annenberg Graduate Fellowship.

1. About Medical Imaging and MRI Scan

Basics of an MRI: MRI scanner can capture images of different organs inside our body in a non-invasive manner without any surgery or insertion. Unlike regular cameras, MRI scanners are not optical devices and rely on the principle of magnetic resonance to capture images. We put the patient in concern, in a very strong magnetic field. The water (H_2O molecule) in a person's body has hydrogen atoms which act like tiny magnets and align along the magnetic field. When such aligned hydrogen atoms are disturbed by external electromagnetic fields (purposefully applied) the Hydrogen atoms start re-aligning themselves with the magnetic field. This process of realigning releases energy that depends on the local microscopic environment of the hydrogen atoms. We record the released energy via several electrical coils over several minutes to gather detailed information, which is then post-processed to get images which a human can understand. This is known as MRI Acquisition.

Computer Vision and Artificial Intelligence are intricately linked with medical research, especially in the area of medical diagnostics using equipments such as MRI imaging, CT scan etc. MRI has inherently low sensitivity (only a small fraction of all hydrogen atoms contribute to the recorded MRI signal images due to quantum mechanical effects) and recorded MRI signals are sensitive to imperfections in MRI system and motion of the patients. This can result into corruption of MRI image such as severe noise, geometrical distortion etc. that can make the task of diagnosis from such images difficult and unreliable.

2. Chitresh's Ph.D Work at the University of Southern California

There are 2 ways in which the problem of getting better and more clear images from MRI scan can be looked at:

- Post-processing the data viz the images taken, so as to produce a more accurate visualisation, from a medical point of view.

- With the help of extensive research, upgrade the algorithms in the equipment to capture better images of the relevant organs, in the first place.

In practice, most researchers largely focus on one of these approaches in their research. Chitresh's research during his PhD was focussed on combining both of these approaches for superior results. Extracting insights from an MRI scan is an overall goal which constitutes multiple subgoals such as improving the quality of image, removing noise etc. His project was specifically concentrated on artifact correction, i.e. removing undesirable appearances in the MRI scan output. He developed several techniques to correct artifacts in a variety of MRI images which include diffusion MRI image, functional MRI images etc. He also made other contributions in this field and his work involved different topics from advanced mathematics under the domain of signal and systems. His PhD thesis can be found in the references section.

3. Problem of Reducing MRI Scan Recall Rate by Clinician

At GE Research, one of the projects Chitresh worked on was aimed at bridging the gap between what results do the doctors want from a particular MRI scan and what the lab technicians, who run the MRI scan, provide. In a usual workflow, doctor may recommend an MRI scan of a body part for a patient. Then an MRI lab technician runs the MRI scan on the patient based on the prescription. However, as the technician is not deeply aware of the patient's health problem and anatomical details inside body, he/she may not run the scan in the most appropriate manner. Lack of proper training for technicians could also cause a similar outcome. Some issues that consequently arise in the MRI scan are i) image not taken at the right orientation or the right plane ii) more focus on one part of organ while less focus on some other key part iii) noise in the images etc. Resultantly, the doctor may not be fully satisfied with the MRI images and thus ask for a re-run of the MRI scan. This leads to losses and inefficiencies, as MRI scans are costly and time-consuming.

Chitresh's work was focused on minimizing this MRI scan repetition rate, which currently stands around twenty percent, a very high number. The solution that GE has developed reduces the technician's overhead of manually finding the exact part of the human organ to be scanned and completely automates it. For example, if a technician's goal is to get a scan of "optic nerve," then he/she just needs to select the organ name (optic nerve in this case) from a drop-down menu. After this, the machine which is pre-trained to locate the correct part will automatically align the images for correct orientation and correct focus.

This is achieved by using a "localizer" image to automatically find all anatomy of interest. Localizer image are like preview in digital cameras – they are coase, low-resolution image, which are seen by the technician when trying to identify the relative anatomical position and locate the part of the body to be scanned. The model behind the localizer image has been pre-trained using a combination of deep learning algorithms and other image processing algorithms to find the exact parts that the technician is supposed to focus on. The pre-training is done on a data of sufficient number of images of every body part. The model can segment the image it is seeing and can infer whether it is the correct part of the organ or not, and based on this, the camera takes the decision whether to shift towards scanning some other part of the organ, or this part only.

The above system has been recently approved by the FDA under the name AIRx™ and should be seeing mass adoption in the near future. The MRI recall rate is expected to go down drastically with this system, though an exact number cannot be estimated right now due to legal compliance.

Here are two videos which explain more about the problem and its solution:

- Video titled 'What's new with GE Healthcare – AIRx.' (web url: https://youtu.be/-BG-xWpQNZY)

- https://www.gehealthcare.com/-/media/75a574cfc32248709517 cc236e89648c.mp4

4. About MTBI Brain Injury: Identification, Diagnosis and Cure

MTBI, as in Mild Traumatic Brain Injury, is a condition that may occur due to repetitive mild injuries to the head. Though any diagnostic results after the injury suffered won't show anything explicitly abnormal, evidence indicates that such successive and repetitive mild injuries across time cause significant damage to the brain resulting in cognitive problems and other types of disabilities and health problems. This problem has occurred quite often in American Football and thus GE Healthcare partnered with NFL, USA (National Football League) to find the cause, diagnosis and cure of such an injury.

The 'head on bumping' move in American football can sometimes cause tearing or strain in the brain muscles without any external or internal bleeding. Current state-of-the-art medical equipments such as CT and MRI machines are unable to detect these injuries and the doctors often end up dismissing the symptoms, experienced and reported by such patients, as trivial. However, when the brains of former NFL players who had passed away were examined in detail, it showed obvious damage and injury.

The first challenge of detection of the injury has been explored by GE Research team. For this, data samples of brain MRI scan of those people who had MTBI was collected across different duration of time after the reporting of symptoms by the patient. Also, datasets of non-MTBI brain MRI scans were added to it. This combined dataset was subjected to rigorous analytics and feature engineering after which it is used to train a model to detect the outlier using a combination of deep learning and Recursive Feature Elimination (RFE) techniques. The algorithms in the MRI machines across the country have been upgraded to incorporate the desirable changes in the way images are taken, along with a lot of post-processing on top of those images, to detect MTBI accurately. Thus we are able to detect if someone has MTBI or not using GE's latest MRI machines. However, the challenge of quantification of the injury is yet to be solved for.

One reference paper: https://www.ncbi.nlm.nih.gov/pubmed/30024343

5. What Are Some Best Practices Followed by GE Healthcare and its Research Team

When it comes to tools and techniques, GE research teams have the freedom to use state-of-the-art technologies in the world, within their legal compliance and policies. They have a very containerization based approach towards their software-based products. The Computer Vision and AI team uses multiple open source libraries and platforms such as pytorch, tensorflow, keras, openCV, openGL, ITK etc. However, each of the open source tools needs to undergo a screening process for legal compliance by appropriate teams before their usage.

Medical research has a very long life cycle with a major share going into regulatory approvals, public adoption etc. A key question that needs to be answered is whether or not the new medical product's success rate is better than the current success rate of doctors, at scale. Regulatory bodies approve the project only after they are fully satisfied with the results. Also, A/B testing in the world of medical diagnostics is often not applicable, because you can't take a risk with patient's health. Pre-trial evaluation of the latest innovations and technology in this domain must be done in such a fashion that it can be adopted across the masses after approval, i.e. the simulations or offline-evaluation should be so thorough that there is near 100% guarantee of the product's success. The next stage is to convince the medical institutions including hospitals and clinicians to adopt the product. The last stage is to gain the trust of the patients themselves about these medical technological products. Each stage can take months or even years to fulfil.

GE Healthcare research team is primarily divided into GE research and GE engineering team. While the former is focussed towards cutting edge research with publications and patents as an end goal, the latter is more inclined towards working on low hanging fruits along with maintenance, upgradation and code changes to the existing firmware and software.

An interesting yet imperative anecdote is regarding the practise at GE research to adhere to strict Government laws such as HIPAA. The law prescribes that any patient-related information cannot be transmitted over the internet and also cannot be shared with the outside world. Hence, while patients' data can be transferred within a medical institution over LAN, it must be transferred hand-to-hand only across institutions or organisations. Further, the information must be anonymized so that researchers and others reading the research articles cannot identify the patient.

6. How Is Deep Learning Impacting Medical Imaging Research

Deep Learning is very relevant in the work of Chitresh and his team. Deep Learning has shown to outperform traditional supervised machine learning algorithms when it comes to media content like images and videos. Hence they are speedily replacing the existing algorithms in this domain. Earlier techniques needed hand tuned features which were time-consuming but deep learning techniques are able to extract representational features from the input data, which is particularly useful for medical imaging problems as medical images have a lot of peculiarities and noise, which are difficult to be captured using handcrafted features.

As deep learning gradually becomes prevalent in the area of medical science and research, this domain will be more and more democratized. People who don't have enough domain knowledge but have an expertise in deep learning techniques are increasingly being hired in these teams across organizations.

Another trend with the advent of deep learning is that problems that were earlier considered too complex to be solved will have a shot taken at now. Deep Learning has enabled researchers to attack such tough problems, like finding the volume of the brain of a human baby before birth, to determine the baby's health. The existing technology such as ultrasound is capable of taking only 2D images but deep learning based segmentation techniques can be used on top of it to obtain a 3D representation of the same.

However, a downside of the adoption of deep learning is that products based on it have lesser interpretability, as it is a black box kind of a solution. Thus it comes down as a burden on the scientists to explain their results from the provided inputs in a proper manner. This will further make it difficult to gain the trust of medical institutions and clinicians for mass adoption. So there is a cost and effort involved in tackling this, along with the obvious 'data hungry-ness' hurdle that deep learning has always faced. Also, in the future, it is expected that there will be a lot of research in the explainability of deep learning and artificial intelligence techniques, which is hoped to boost its usage in the healthcare industry.

7. Difference Between Research in Ph.D vs in Industry

According to Chitresh, The Ph.D is somewhat more geared towards publications, which typically bring forward new theoretical ideas that may not have immediate practical application. The grants from the colleges, universities, government agencies etc. are typically used for such publication oriented research.

But, in areas like Computer Vision a lot of grants have started coming from industries and private organizations like Microsoft, Facebook etc. Therefore the deliverables have also changed from mere publications to that of having a more immediate bearing in the real world. Industry is focussed more towards application-driven research. Here a larger share of focus is on short span projects with a typically 3–5 years horizon, with the rest going into long term projects with a typically 10–20 years horizon.

8. How Is Data Handled at Scale at GE Research

The scale at which GE Research handles data is significant. In the field of medical imaging, number of data points are usually small, as one data point often refers to one patient. Furthermore, only a small population in the world has access to MRI machines, and even among them many may disagree to share their test results for research purposes. Hence a dataset obtained from MRI imaging is from a pool of size usually not exceeding 50,000 patients. However, the size of each data point (an MRI image) is huge (in gigabytes), and hence managing the entire data set becomes non-trivial. Hence the data preprocessing stage is done with distributed memory architecture based data systems like hadoop and spark. However modelling, training etc components of research is done using shared memory architecture i.e. using a single node/machine, as the cutting edge mathematical techniques of this domain, can be currently implemented only on such systems. Deployment of models is also done on shared memory frameworks as only 1 sample needs to be handled at a time.

Because the scale of data is huge, a lot of time goes into data handling and processing. Approximately 50% of effort goes into data collection, storage, cleaning, processing, labelling and annotation. The remaining 50% of effort goes into applying mathematical techniques and algorithms, customized or standard, and then evaluating the results.

9. Advice to Candidates Aspiring to Join GE Research

GE Research team has roles across different levels. While candidates with Ph.D degree can join directly at senior positions, graduates and postgraduates can join at entry level and then climb up with experience. What's must is a very deep fundamental understanding of Machine Learning, Deep Learning or other mathematical techniques one has used before? It is good, though not compulsory, to have knowledge of physics of imaging. The team here believes that coding is just a way of expressing a mathematical idea and thus interviews for roles in his team are not particularly focussed on coding skills in any specific programming language. However, candidates are rigorously tested on their logical reasoning abilities.

It is worth mentioning here that there is a separate engineering team for GE Healthcare which is involved in the deployment and maintenance of products developed by the research team. This team is interested in hiring software engineers and the interview process deeply involves much stronger coding skills, algorithms and data structures.

MakeMyTrip
Madhu Gopinathan

Author: Pulkit Bansal

About the Company

MakeMyTrip is India's largest online travel platform, and it provides online flight, hotel, cabs, and homestays booking facility. The Indian online travel market is growing at a rapid pace and is expected to touch 13.6 billion dollars by 2021 which would be roughly 43% of the entire travel industry in India (Praxis global report). Already well known for booking flights, the company has recently focused a lot of attention on Hotels. Though only 15–20% hotel bookings in India happen via online channel at present, this number is expected to greatly increase in the coming few years. During the last one year, MakeMyTrip had more than 1.5 Cr hotel room-nights sold on its online platforms (company's annual reports).

Brief Biography

Madhu Gopinathan heads the Data Science team at MakeMyTrip. He has previously been associated with two startups, one of which led to an IPO. He has also worked at Infosys, Microsoft, and Sun Microsystems in the past. He has completed an MS in Computer Science from the University of Florida Gainesville, and a PhD in Computer Science from Indian Institute of Science Bangalore.

1. My View of Data Science in Industry

In industry, hunting for the right data to solve your problem is quite important. The relevant data you require may sometimes not even be available, and one needs to work with data team to start logging all the relevant information. Also, the data may be scattered across different places, and you may need to build various pipelines to combine all the data in a usable form.

One also needs the skill of formulating a business problem into a Data Science problem. But you don't have a lot of time, and you need to move fast. We follow the approach of building a baseline model first and then iteratively improve it.

2. Machine Learning Problems at MakeMyTrip

There are two chief categories of problems: (a) Improve customer experience e.g. chatbots for customer support, personalized hotel recommendations (b) Improve efficiency: inventory management, dynamic pricing, computing credit-worthiness of a customer for booking on loan.

3. Culture of Data Science at MMT

At MakeMyTrip, we have a single Data Science team which interacts with various parts of the company. Our primary focus is on solving business problems, and not research problems. At MakeMyTrip, we have a very high degree of interaction with the product managers, who guide us on understanding the problem's business value, and the final objective which we want to optimize for.

The DS-problems can be long term e.g. improving hotel recommendations where we've been working for over a year, and short term e.g. when a product manager requires a quick-model for an urgent product release. A Data Scientist is expected to do everything from building data pipelines, model development, and deploying it into production (he may be assisted by some core-engineers though).

One of the challenges for us is how to iterate faster on models. Towards this, we're exploring new tools that can make life easier for our Data Scientists. Simplifying and automating the data gathering, pipelining, and data quality-checking procedure is an important focus area for us as a team. Another thing we're looking to do is fine tuning the engagement model with the core-engineering teams and providing them training on basics of machine learning, so that elementary models can be built by the larger-engineering team, and only the advanced-models or "model refinement" part would eventually come to the Data Science team.

4. The Hotel Recommendation Problem

At MakeMyTrip, there are over 50k domestic hotels and 5,00,000+ international hotels. Therefore we want to make the job of finding a suitable hotel as easy as possible for every user. When a user is searching for hotels, we would like to show the most relevant hotels on the top of the list. To do this we should ideally rank the hotels in decreasing order of probability of being booked by the user.

The key performance metric in hotel ranking algorithm is that of conversion i.e. number of hotel bookings per 100 users who are coming on the platform.

Relevance of hotels can be inferred from several signals:

- Hotel quality (review ratings, no. of past bookings/clicks, MMT assured or not, ...)

- Query (city, adults, children, check-in, check-out, ...)

- Device (hardware, OS, browser, ...)

- User History (bookings, cancellations, reviews, ...)

- Recent funnel activity (views, filters/sorts applied, ...)

Our initial model was rule-based and basically a linear combination of several hotel-specific features. This model was greatly improved upon by a personalized hotel-recommendation model based on a novel implementation of the collaborative-filtering idea. It basically considers user's past bookings and shows hotels similar to it (inferred from preferences of similar users i.e. those who have booked the same hotel(s) as the current user). This resulted in significant improvement in conversion.[1]

Now we are trying to further improve this model by building a single framework that can take hundreds of different features into account including query-based, past user bookings, user's recent behaviour, and hotel specific features. We are using "Learning To Rank" techniques for this. We're experimenting with both gradient boosted tree (LambdaMART) and neural network based approaches.

There are several aspects which make the ranking problem particularly challenging. Although conversion is important, increasing the revenue per user is also a key business goal. These goals can sometimes conflict i.e. you may achieve high conversion by showing just budget hotels, but that would lead to a decrease in revenue.

Another thing to note is that, typical ranking algorithms tend to show the same set of top-selling hotels to every customer. Due to this newer hotels may not get any chance, and we would never discover potential "hero-hotels." Also, lack of click or book data on these hotels may make it impossible to rank them correctly. This can be formulated as an "exploration-exploitation" problem. The challenge here is to keep showing high-performing hotels most of the time (exploitation), but also take calculated risks and collect data by giving some opportunity to newer hotels (exploration), with the goal to optimize conversion in the long term.

5. Dynamic Pricing Problem

Dynamic Pricing is a strategy where prices change in real-time considering supply, demand, competitor-pricing, and user-need/behaviour. These models are used to tailor pricing for customer segments by simulating how targeted customers will respond to any price changes. It's important to note that dynamic pricing isn't just about raising the prices – it often involves lowering them.[2]

Along with profit maximisation, building such engine helped us to understand market trends, helped hoteliers to clear out their slow moving inventory, and even helped our customers to pick bookings based on the prices they are willing to pay.

We take a contextual multi-armed bandit approach for this problem. The model learns the optimal pricing by intelligently searching over the pricing space and analyzes user reaction patterns induced as a result of this pricing. It then iteratively adjusts the pricing until it reaches the optimal point for all the parties involved (i.e. the customers, hoteliers, and us).

6. NLP and Chatbots

We have currently built a chatbot for post-sales customer enquiry e.g. helping them with queries such as finding correct airport terminals, cancel flight bookings, or find out baggage-information.

The basic principle of our chatbot is to predict customer's intent from their chat message. We're using word and sentence embeddings based NLP techniques for intent-prediction. The data we collect from the interactions of users with chatbot can tell us how well we're performing on each intent. Wherever the bot doesn't do well, we can supply those data points with correct labels as additional feedback to the chatbot model so that its performance on those intents can also improve.

We've also worked on a hotel "review-mining" project. Here based on hotel-reviews we were able to construct tags for hotels e.g. "good-breakfast," "near the beach" etc. A user can discover such a hotel if he types relevant keywords in the search box.

7. Who Is a Good Data Scientist?

Firstly, one needs to have strong fundamentals. E.g. for logistic regression why we have a certain form for the cost function? Could you code up gradient descent from scratch? One should not look at models as just black boxes, and being a library-level Data Scientist is not enough. One should have some understanding of what's going on inside the model. Also, a good understanding of the foundations of statistics is important. In addition, principles of A/B testing, designing appropriate metrics are also important.

To work in industry one must be a good programmer. You should be hands-on with tools like python, SQL, and numpy/pandas libraries. We also like to see some experience with production level engineering because most of the models we develop in the e-commerce setting are directly served in real time to live customers. Therefore we take latency of the code very seriously, and it is important to write clean modular code. We use the open-source tool Airflow for scheduling pipeline jobs, and for databases we use Hive and Amazon-Redshift.

Apart from the technical skills we also value some personality traits. I think curiosity and being self-driven is crucial. One should be able to unearth insights from data. Communication with product managers and understanding business context is also quite important to be effective in our company.

For people new to Data Science, although it is good to do a course to get a basic knowledge of the concepts, but it doesn't tell about how much you've absorbed and how much you can apply. By building a GitHub portfolio of your work, or writing articles on a blog one can better demonstrate his potential.

We are open for jobs, and also for internships (at least 4 months).

8. How Online Travel Industry Will Change in the Coming Few Years?

India is the fastest growing major economy in the world. As the economy grows, travel is bound to increase – both business and leisure travel. Therefore, the prospects look pretty good for the industry. Natural Language/voice-based search, especially in Indian languages will a big breakthrough in the travel industry and we expect it to be widely adopted in the within the next few years.

References

1. *Hotel Price Recommendation @ MMT*, https://medium.com/makemytrip-engineering/hotel-price-recommendation-mmt-14a6577ce95d

2. *The "My" in MakeMyTrip: How Per-User Personalization Boosted Conversion at MMT*, https://medium.com/makemytrip-engineering/personalized-hotel-ranking-using-past-interaction-data-1a5434508635

BSES Rajdhani Power Limited
Rajesh Bansal

Authors: Pulkit Bansal, Pankaj Gupta

About the Company:

BSES Rajdhani Power Limited (BRPL) is a joint venture company of the Reliance Group and Govt of Delhi. BRPL distributes power in West and South of Delhi and presently serving to almost 2.5 million consumers. In 2006, BRPL introduced 100% Electronic meter data download which was quite unique at that time. In 2010, BRPL became a leading player in electronic meter data analytics. Today BRPL is recognised as a utility with successful track record of loss reduction, reliability improvement and correct technology adoption.

Brief Biography:

Rajesh Bansal is currently the Head of Network Operations at BSES Delhi. In the last 10 years, he has developed many analytics programs to detect theft, network health, loss reduction and to analyze consumer behaviour in the power sector. He has shared his experience and concept in more than 20 countries, with utilities, policy makers, students and industry. In India, he is also the Chairman of CBIP Metering Standardization Committee. Previously, he was the head of first Single phase Electronic meter manufacturing company in India. Rajesh Bansal has done his graduation in Electronic Engineering in 1985 from NITK Surathkal, and started his career as a Scientist at ISRO Satellite Centre.

1. About Our Business

We are in the electricity distribution business, and our main goal is to meet the consumer energy demand with efficiency and reliability. We do not generate electricity ourselves but we buy it from other public or private generation companies. We want to reduce our cost of power and losses such as technical, theft/distribution loss and collection loss (e.g. customer not paying by due date). We also want to ensure continuous availability of optimum supply.

The main priorities for our company are (a) reduce loss and optimize the cost of buying electricity (b) timely fix network failure or transformer problems (c) tackle non-availability of supply. For us, power outage is a lost opportunity and thus is a big deal, e.g. if even for 15 min there is no electricity due to any fault, we lose heavily since we won't get paid for that time.

2. A Peek Into Our Data Science Problems

In my view analytics is always done for an objective, which defines some expectation or minimizes some undesirable issues.

As such electricity in large volume cannot be stored and it cannot be destroyed, therefore our supply should match with the demand which varies continuously. Therefore accurately predicting future electricity demand is important for us. We need to dynamically adjust the amount of electricity to buy based on current demand and prices.

A related problem for us is to buy electricity at the cheapest rate possible. Electric Power also has exchanges which matches the sellers and buyers of electricity, which are very similar to stock market exchanges. In countries like Singapore, a lot of transactions are done for pure speculation i.e. with an intent of pure money making by betting on electricity prices. This market is quite big, and if you can consistently predict power prices ahead of time then indeed Utility can make additional money!!

Cost of power is made of

1. **Long Term** component which a power distribution company has agreed to buy over a long period of time.

2. **Spot** component where the power distribution company specifies its power requirements to the generator-company every 15 min slot for next one day.

3. **Instant** component is used to manage the surplus or deficit of power at the time of distribution. The power is bought and sold at the price of that time.

For predicting demand, we use the last few years of time series data. Some pattern is carried from history, and the rest comes from the most recent days. Typically there are 20–30 tricky days out of 365, rest are not very hard to predict. Weather is a very important factor, and taking it into account is crucial for us. Earlier we had a few MBA graduates in our team, who used to build models on Excel. They used to build a weighted linear model based on a list of parameters/factors on which the demand depends.

At present we have outsourced this problem to an external company who are building the models for us. We predict demand at every 15 min interval. Demand varies greatly by the time of the day/date/festivals/occasions/weather patterns etc. Sometimes the demand can depend on the outcome of unpredictable events e.g. if today India wins the semi-final match, then two days from now everyone will turn on the TV to see the final, but if India loses the power demand will be lower.

Renewable energy is the cheapest source of energy but is very unpredictable. If renewable energy is available then it's our first preference. Accurately forecasting the amount of power generated by renewable sources is a challenging problem, but if solved this could enormously improve our business efficiency.

The instant rate can vary a lot with time. There is an additional penalty if actual off take varies a lot with defined schedule causing surplus/shortage position in the grid. A good thumb rule is: buy extra if you expect a shortage in the exchange, and under-schedule if power is expected to be surplus i.e. buy later at instant rate.

3. Challenges in Our Industry

Fault detection is a crucial problem. If one could detect catastrophic failure e.g. sparking or fire in advance it can be immensely useful. One could do this by analyzing the change in the characteristic of input/output voltage or network faults. If the gap between input and output voltage increases suddenly, this implies loose connection/sparking. Analytics can help with (a) detection of fault (b) cause of fault (c) remedial action. There is a big demand for being able to analyze equipment failure and capacity projection. This can be done based on (1) Failure history (2) Instantaneous reasons, which could be hard to find.

We need to have a system of "timely warning" and "timely replacement," because we can't wait to fix it until the failure happens. We need to capture the trend: i.e. measure critical parameters of the network assets and predict what repair/replacement is required. For this, we need historical data. Even if some specific data is missing, we can start collecting it now, so that in future we can do it better. It is never too late to start!

4. About Revenue Leakage and Electricity Theft and Complaint Management

To analyze electricity theft we measure the energy gap between sending and receiving end, and plot this graph wrt time. Sending end means the reading at the transformers which is distributing the power to an area while receiving end is the sum-total of the energy usage of that area based on meter-readings. The gaps are acceptable to a threshold, but when the gap is too high it means distribution system have an abnormality.

Suppose we see a pattern where in a household every night at 7:00 pm there is a drop in electricity consumption relative to other houses in the neighbourhood. It might mean that the house residents routinely leave the house to go somewhere. Or it could mean that the house is doing fraud by getting the power directly through wire.

While predicting theft, we need close to 100% accuracy. We cannot afford to be wrong here, because the person who is innocent can file a defamation case creating huge trouble for the company.

Another interesting DS application in case of customer service-

1. The power distributors receive complaints/calls from several sources like phone, mail, chat, sms, etc.

2. Check the pattern of calls to detect the seriousness and scale of the issue.

3. Optimize the power distribution to ensure the minimum case of complaint-neglection.

5. The History of Analytics in Our Industry

In India, we started anomaly detection as far back as 2006–07, because we were collecting a lot of meter data. People were amazed when we used to tell them how many fans/ACs/rooms they have in their house without getting inside their homes. We could figure it out purely based on electricity consumption data. Countries like the US and Germany had mechanical meters at that time. Only in 2009–10 they got better meters. We were leading the field earlier, but with the new AI/ML wave and availability of data now everyone has been able to catch-up.

In the current scenario, predicting anomaly is not enough, you also need to predict when that anomaly is going to occur. With domain knowledge you can say detect only 'N' kinds of anomalies, but not a new $(N+1)^{th}$ anomaly. We need a way to analyze "event to event correlation," and its trend. Everything within limit is okay, but we're not detecting the trend when this limit might be exceeded

6. Who Is a Good Data-Analyst for This Domain?

I believe that "Data is what has happened," and "Analytics is a tool to drive information keeping in view an objective." The objective for power distribution can be efficiency improvement i.e. lower power cost, lower T & D loss, lower operation cost and better services, demand forecasting and network optimization or Power Reliability improvement ie lower failure, fast outage management, fault predictions etc.

Analytics is a tool which converts data into objective oriented information. A Good data analyst is one:

- Who understand what all data is available and the meaning of that data.
- Should know the main and micro objective of distribution companies.
- Can understand how sub-activity can help to achieve the main objective.
- Has the ability to reason with information in various forms: analysis, prediction, and pictorial display.

It is strongly recommended that the analyst should have good knowledge of various analytics tools and power-distribution domain. He should try to learn so as he can make a better relation between data and objective.

7. Conclusions and Future of Analytics in Our Industry

I feel that analytics should reach every home and dynamic rates should be allowed. In India, there is a fixed tariff for the whole time, but few countries have already started with a dynamic rate system for certain category of consumers. If you use equipment at higher demand time you'll pay more, otherwise less. This will make the consumer plan ahead of time and we'll get a more uniform electricity consumption across the day rather than all of it happening at a fixed time. This will make the market more efficient and better for everyone.

There is also demand response problem. For e.g. a seller is unable to meet its contract, because it won't have enough electricity generation, then they can modify the contract e.g. say I'll cut 5 hours of electricity in a month of my choice. But for this option, the seller will need to compensate the buyer appropriately.

Predicting location-based demand is another upcoming problem. Soon electric vehicles are going to take over and it is expected that within the next 10 years the majority of vehicles will be electric in India. Therefore there is a need to predict time-varying demand at various locations e.g. near home or office, for this "mobile load."

Data analytics can help us better manage customer complaints. Complaints are received from various sources like phone, email, sms, chat, etc. We can predict the traffic from each of these sources and assign the resources proportionally. In case, we have a limit on resources for managing the complaints, using data analytics we can distribute power in such a way that complaints received lies within the constrained-limit. Additionally, some of the complaints can be managed automatically without the involvement of human effort. Looking at the area distribution of the complaints, we can also predict the seriousness of the issue in each of the areas and accordingly prioritize the complaint-resolution process.

WorldQuant
Pulkit Bansal

Authors: Pulkit Bansal, Pankaj Gupta

About WorldQuant:

WorldQuant is an international hedge fund and quantitative investment management firm. Founded in 2007, the firm is currently managing approximately $5 billion in assets under management via quantitative trading. WorldQuant has more than 20 offices in 15 countries including India, Vietnam, South Korea, Russia, Romania, Thailand, Hungary, Israel, China, and Bulgaria. As of April 2017, WorldQuant had more than 500 employees and 450 paid research consultants.

Brief Biography:

Pulkit Bansal is a former Quantitative Researcher at WorldQuant. He started his career in finance industry with Goldman Sachs before moving to quantitative trading at WorldQuant. He graduated at the top of his class from IIT Kanpur in 2012 with an M.Sc. Integrated degree in Mathematics and Scientific Computing. Currently, he is working as a Lead Data Scientist at MakeMyTrip, an online travel company based out of India.

1. What Is the Business of WorldQuant?

The goal of WorldQuant is to generate profits by using quantitative investment and trading strategies. Historically, stock trading has been done manually by a trader who constantly takes multiple "human-decisions" like which stock to transact, when to transact, and in what quantity, based on market patterns, financial news and company information. In contrast at WorldQuant, the trading-decisions are made by fully automated data-driven algorithms, which are also called alphas.

2. What Exactly Is an Alpha?

Alpha is basically an algorithm or a rule that tells when and how much to buy/sell a stock based on market patterns. It is a piece of code which runs periodically e.g. once a day in the morning, and tells us how to allocate money to various stocks in the market (such as NSE in India, Nikkei 225 for Japan). An alpha takes historical stock related data into consideration and, based on that, it tells us how to manage our *portfolio* i.e. the set of stocks and their quantities one possess. A crude example of such a rule could be: if a stock's price increases buy more of it, and if it decreases sell it, and do this in proportion to the percentage change in price in last 1 day. One can easily code-up this rule and then a machine can take decisions and update the portfolio as per the rule everyday.

Now, a good alpha is created by discovering a market signal that ensures high returns and low volatility (variance of daily returns) of the stock portfolio. High returns imply more profits, and low volatility implies more consistency, or in other words, lower risk.

The primary metric used to judge the performance of an alpha is called **"sharpe-ratio,"** which is the ratio of "annual returns" and "annual volatility." A good alpha should have high sharpe ratio. Another desirable property is to have **"low turnover"** i.e. not changing too much of your portfolio too soon, because that would result in paying a lot of transaction fee (the exchange charges you a small fee each time you buy or sell any stock). As a thumb rule, an alpha is quite good if it can consistently predict whether a stock will go up or down more than 55% of the time, and has daily turnover below 15%. A good way to reduce volatility (i.e. risk) is to diversify the portfolio among various stocks rather than concentrating all the money into a few stocks.

An alpha can add value for the company, only if it differs from the existing alphas already present in the alpha pool. For this reason, an alpha is only accepted if the correlation of its daily historical returns with that of all the existing alphas in the system is less than a threshold (low-correlation alpha). Else it is discarded.

3. Setup of WorldQuant's Research & Investment Division

At WorldQuant, researchers, portfolio managers and technologists work towards rigorously identifying sources of alpha i.e. trading signals to generate high profits. The setup consists of a 3-level hierarchy

- **Level 1: Quant Researcher** who discovers new alphas and writes code for them using various financial datasets. His goal is to create as many low-correlation & good alphas as possible, and his rewards depend on the performance of his alphas. Though the researcher builds the alphas, he doesn't have the authority to invest money in those alphas. Those decisions are made by Portfolio Managers.

- **Level 2: Portfolio Manager (PM)** who allocates actual trading capital to different alphas in the alpha-pool and builds a portfolio out of it. They construct strategies using the alphas as building blocks. They may choose alphas depending on which are more favoured by the current market environment, and remove those which are no longer relevant or profitable. Their bonuses are dependent on the performance of their strategies.

- **Level 3: Capital Allocator** system that divides company's capital among different Portfolio Managers. How this is done is a top-level secret, but a better performing portfolio manager is definitely given more money to invest.

A newly hired Data Scientist in World Quant joins at level 1.

4. Incentive and Bonus Structure at WorldQuant

In order to understand how WorldQuant works, it is extremely important to understand the bonus and incentive-system. One needs to appreciate that everything is fundamentally driven by a desire to make higher profits. This is the one rule that remains constant.

The bonuses form the major component of the overall pay of a Quantitative Researcher. A Researcher earns a percentage cut from the profits made as a result of his alphas, and as he grows senior, this percentage cut increases. Another thing to note is that in each year one earns bonus from all the work they have done till that point. E.g. if you made an alpha 5 years back and it is still making a profit, then this year also you'll get a percentage cut from its profit, and since you are more senior now this cut will be bigger than before. This kind of incentive structure motivates people to stay in the company for long term.

For Portfolio managers, the incentive structure is quite similar. It is just that they deal with real money as decided by the Capital Allocator. Their bonus is a percentage cut from the actual profits they make from their strategy (which is a dynamic combination of many alphas) on their allocated capital. To make a higher bonus, a PM's strategy should make good profits, which incentivizes them to use high quality alphas. This in turn gives higher weightage to best-performing alphas of researchers, and therefore better researchers make a higher bonus.

5. How Alphas Are Built?

A Quant Researcher has a variety of financial data at his disposal. They have price and volume data of stocks, twitter data, financial news data, stock-analysts data, earnings call held by companies, holdings of CEOs in companies, economic events feed etc. Quant Researchers are free to use any tool or technique to create new alphas. The techniques can range from simple signals observed from data (e.g. P/E ratio) to advanced neural-networks based models.

Some Examples of Alphas Are

1. Predict the future price of a stock by analysis of price/volume time-series data of stocks. Then build an alpha that buys/sells those stocks whose price is expected to increase/decrease.

2. Use the difference between average of daily high and low prices and daily close price as stock weights.

3. Pair trading and mean reversion: Based on the observation that the stocks of similar companies tend to behave similarly. An alpha can be built from stocks where we observe sudden deviations in the behaviour of similar stocks.

4. Alphas based on options data, and conference-call/stock-dividend data.

5. Alphas built using fundamental data from the company's annual reports such as price to earnings ratio, and many others.

6. News Data: Do sentiment analysis of news text-data to quantify investor's confidence in the health of various stocks. Make a strategy that buys/sells those with high positive/negative sentiments.

7. Technical indicators such as Bollinger Bands, MACD built on stock price data.

The alphas are trained and evaluated using a process called **back-testing** on previous years of data. One way to do this is as follows: Say in the past 5 years of data first 4 years can be used for training, and the last 1 year for testing. Using the historical data of each stock's performance one can compute what returns an alpha would have given (if it were used) on each day in the past data.

But before putting real money into an alpha, portfolio managers would like to be assured that the alpha doesn't just perform well on the past data (where one can also do over-fitting), but it also performs in the current market conditions.

For this reason, once an alpha is trained and submitted, it is frozen and the results are observed in the live stock market. After freezing an alpha, the code cannot be modified. Only when an alpha consistently does well, portfolio managers gain confidence to bet money on it. Portfolio managers typically start with a small amount of money in any alpha, and as they gain more confidence in the consistency of its performance, they increase the money invested on that alpha.

One important point to note about trading is that in order to analyze "how good an alpha is," you don't need to invest real money into it. Since we can get the returns of each stock directly from the market, the returns of an alpha can be computed without betting actual money on it (because an alpha is just a combination of individual stocks).

6. Culture of Data Science at WorldQuant

At WorldQuant your bonus is directly dependent on the performance of your alphas, and this fact motivates you to put your best efforts into building good alphas. When a Quant Researcher joins WorldQuant, he is assigned an advisor (who is a senior experienced employee) to help him get started and know about the details of the system. The advisor also has an incentive to help the researcher, since he gets a percentage cut from the advisee's bonus.

In order to learn about new alphas, one can start with reading finance research papers but in most cases, those ideas don't directly work. This is because if an idea were really profitable, it will be quickly implemented by others and it will no longer be profitable. Also, nobody will tell you anything that will directly make money for you. If he knew it, wouldn't he first make money for himself? Therefore, though research papers can provide some inspiration or teach you a few techniques, it is left to the researcher himself to intelligently use those ideas on his datasets to finally build a profitable alpha.

One downside (or upside) in this industry is a very high focus on "individual achievement." Since your alphas decide your bonus, and because once an alpha is submitted to the system no-one else can submit a "similar alpha," it becomes important for people to keep their ideas a secret. People want to avoid the risk that others might use their idea and submit an alpha before them, and thereby generate profits for themselves. Sometimes people work together in small teams (typically 2–3 people), and divide the total bonus earned by the team among themselves.

The industry is highly competitive, and there is little scope for mediocrity. In order to survive in this industry, you must demonstrate that you have the potential to build a lot of good quality alphas within a relatively short span of time. The motivation to perform comes from two things (1) desire to make a bigger bonus (2) fear of the consequences of poor performance. It wouldn't be wrong to say that, this industry truly believes in implementing the rule "hire slow and fire fast."

7. What Are Some of the Major Challenges You Faced While Working in WorldQuant?

Firstly, finding new insights from data and converting them into alphas is itself a challenge. One has to move faster than others. The challenge is to discover a signal from the data that others in the market don't know about, and use it to generate profits. Only then one can "beat-the-market." If an insight is well-known in the market, then no money can be made using it, because the stock price will always reflect it immediately.

Money in the market is made by taking advantage of market inefficiencies, and markets are close to 100% efficient. Also, old alphas die with time, and as more people discover them, they are no longer profitable. In other words, that inefficiency no longer exists in the system. So, one has to consistently hunt for new alphas and look at new datasets.

Another challenge is to automate the process of generating new alphas, i.e. a machine can itself find trends in the market. Such alphas are known as "machine alphas" in contrast to "human alphas." Algorithms such as genetic algorithms are used in this area, but often such alphas suffer from overfitting. Though building such a system is not easy, there is a lot of scope for further research & development in this area.

8. What Is Your Advice for Students Who Are Aspiring to Join WorldQuant?

WorldQuant looks to hire people with a solid academic background, and with a degree from a top-tier college. Having very strong quantitative skills is a must for entering this field. It's not necessary to be a star programmer, but one should have the ability to convert an idea in mind to a piece of code. It is assumed that the candidates can learn the finer details of programming or tech-skills during the job. It is not a prerequisite to have a knowledge of investing or finance to join WorldQuant. However, having some knowledge might help in getting started fast in the role.

Another important thing is the ability to handle stress. This is because creating new alphas at a fast pace is a reasonably demanding task. Although nobody orders you, new-joiners routinely put 12 to 14 hours a day to build alphas. The very best performers consistently put 80 to 100 hours of work per week.

In order to be good at the job, one needs to be self-driven and have the desire to go the extra-mile. Also one has to be highly "result oriented." At WorldQuant, nobody gives you any instructions or looks at what effort are you putting in everyday. You are solely judged based on the performance of your alphas.

9. Does This Kind of Work Serve Any Purpose in This World or Is It Just Money Making?

Although Quantitative Traders are purely driven by the desire to make more money, in this pursuit, they unintentionally benefit the world as well. Here is an explanation behind this argument.

In order to make money for themselves, Quantitative Traders must invest their money into potentially more profitable companies and pull out money from loss-making ones. Thus they are giving opportunities to high calibre people who will potentially create value for the world by pushing money into their ventures, and they are also bearing the risk.

Another point worth noting is that, this industry disproportionately rewards those who are the first to recognize a future star e.g. if someone had invested $100,000 in Google in 1998 he would be a billionaire by now. Therefore every trader has an incentive to "move fast," and to "seize the opportunity before others." This market dynamics, in turn, helps support the rapid pace of growth and innovation in our world.

Reliance Jio
Dr. Shailesh Kumar

Authors: Pulkit Bansal, Srijan Saket

About Reliance Jio:

Reliance Jio Infocomm Limited is the third largest mobile network operator in India with over 250 million subscribers. The company commercially launched its services in September 2016 and within six months it crossed 100 million subscribers. This is the fastest ramp-up by any mobile network operator anywhere in the world.

Brief Biography:

Dr. Shailesh Kumar is currently the Chief Data Scientist at Reliance Jio. He has over twenty years of experience in applying and innovating machine learning, statistical pattern recognition, and data mining algorithms to hard prediction problems in a wide variety of domains. He has been an invited speaker at TEDx, NASSCOM, UNESCO, Times Group and HasGeek among others. He is also a Visiting Faculty at Indian School of Business. He has completed his PhD in Computer Engineering from The University of Texas at Austin. He has previously worked at Ola, Google, Microsoft Bing, Yahoo! Labs and FICO Research.

1. Building AI for India

At present, there is no AI stack for India specific use cases. There are very good AI stacks available for Western or Chinese problems. But nothing substantial in raw or processed format is available for India.

In this space there are broadly four problems we are targeting:

1. **Speech for India:** India is a country with many languages. There are many people who converse in their regional/local languages. There are not many ML solutions which can parse these languages and give useful insights. There is an additional difficulty layer of different accents to this problem. If we compare this problem to languages like English/Chinese, huge advancements have been made in order to solve the speech problem.

2. **Language Stack (Including Machine Translation):** If we see the history of NLP, most of the developments have come from English datasets. There are many tools e.g. WordNet available to understand English text but the same is not true for Indian languages. Also, very little data for Indian languages is available digitally on any platform.

3. **Computer Vision for India:** Although this is largely a culture-independent problem, the western datasets may not contain India-specific objects (e.g. bullock cart, auto rickshaw). Similarly, for facial recognition problem, the models trained on Chinese or American faces do not work well in the Indian context.

4. **Knowledge Graph:** There is a need to build a universal knowledge graph specifically for the Indian context. This would solve many problems related to the Indian context, or any concept around which the knowledge graph is built, for that matter. This will give us a general representation of the problems and would lead us to a futuristic goal of "General AI."

Let me now introduce the concept of knowledge graph and how it can help us in solving the problems mentioned above.

2. Knowledge Graph

We may think that data is the primary thing for building models, but actually it's not the case. Rather the knowledge/process or system that generates the data is most important. The world is made up of entities, attributes, events and relationships between them.

Knowledge graph is a way of representing data as a graph where the nodes are various entities, and the edges represent relationships between the entities. Google and Microsoft Bing have already built a knowledge graph. This is a more fundamental way of doing Machine Learning than neural networks or LSTM etc.

Let us look at an example of machine translation. The current models are all probabilistic, but we should question whether the idea of "probability of a sequence of words" is even meaningful or not. How do humans translate? We take a text and convert this into a knowledge representation and then translate. For e.g. for the Hindi sentence "ईंट का जवाब पत्थर से,"

a typical translation may be more of a literal one e.g. "The answer of brick with stone," but a more appropriate translation might be "Tit for Tat." (I've explained this in more detail in my talk "towards thinking machines" on YouTube)

I believe that rather than "word embeddings" (e.g. Word2Vec) we need "sense embeddings." Two sentences in different languages that mean the same thing should have the same sense embeddings. The current embeddings are not "cross-language." The success of these word embeddings could be just some lucky statistical flukes.

Knowledge is a language independent way of saying the same thing. E.g. "Delhi is the capital of India" or "Dilli bharat ki rajdhani hai" both have the same meaning. Any statement we encounter is not just words but knowledge. When we read a document we don't remember the words or sentences but the meaning and knowledge we gain out of it. This leads us to a two-step approach to machine translation

1. **Language Analysis:** Convert sentence into knowledge.

2. **Language Synthesis:** Go from Language1 to knowledge, and then knowledge to Language2.

3. State of AI in India, Research and What I Would Like to See More in India

We're facing several roadblocks in India

1. Lack of resources or data: In China/US a lot of work has gone into building language resources e.g. WordNet/POS Tagger etc.

2. In Indian languages, even basic parsers are not available.

3. Very little data on the web specifically for the Indian context.

4. Parallel corpus i.e. same set of sentences translated in two different languages is lacking for Indian languages for machine translation. E.g. Gujarati to Punjabi how much data do we really have? Close to nothing.

For machine translation, the deep learning method requires a parallel corpus of data i.e. where we have a set of sentences translated word-by-word from one language into another. In India, we wish to build a universal translator that can work for any pair of languages. To achieve this, it is not possible for us to take the deep learning approach since it is very data hungry. With so many different languages in India just collecting enough data will take enormous effort.

To understand the difficulty more concretely, just imagine that it took us four years to collect 50,000 sentence-pairs (translated between two languages), which is not enough. In comparison, the knowledge graph approach requires much less data. Therefore we wish to use it to develop tools or understand the conversations, preferences etc. for the Indian context more closely.

In India, in research work I see the following main problems:

- Mostly incremental/application work happening.

- Real innovation is not happening.

- Profound contributions or ideas are not coming out.

4. Different Approaches to Model Building

People have been glorifying deep learning in recent years, especially since the success of ImageNet. But there are many other alternatives. When it comes to model building there are two mindsets:

1. **Model-Centric:** Use lots of data and compute (word embeddings/ imagenets are examples), and model has to do the hard work. In the end, the model is highly un-interpretable and complex.

2. **Domain Knowledge Oriented:** E.g. Knowledge graph and others where we carefully build features and do a lot of feature engineering. Even at Google, for some of the problems, they still use logistic regression on a very powerful set of features

When building any model following are some important considerations:

1. How will this model perform in a data-poor environment

2. Is this the way humans do it? (accuracy is a secondary concern)

Many of the AI systems of today are in some sense brute force i.e. we just throw lots of data and compute power. One has to understand that deep Learning is not the answer to every question. It should be used primarily when it is not possible to do handcrafted feature engineering with data (e.g. images). In contrast, bayesian probabilistic learning is a very elegant way of doing things.

5. Problems at Reliance Industries

At Reliance we are looking at several major classes of problems:

1. **Factories and Refinery:** Our Jamnagar refinery is the world's largest oil refinery. It has many complex parts. Everyone has specialized understanding of some parts, but nobody grasps it completely. This problem is from Industrial IOT domain and we have several problems such as (a) How to improve the plant's efficiency? (b) parts' failure detection and prediction (using sensor data) (c) Scheduling maintenance. We have 10 years of sensor data for temperature/pressure/past failures, which we are using to tackle these challenges.

2. **Telecom Sector:** Reliance Jio is the largest network in the world with over 250 million customers. One of the key challenges is to optimally adapt a mobile network with static towers to meet dynamic demands (e.g. people living in office during the day versus at home during the night). Some aspects of these towers are programmatically controllable, and we want to dynamically adjust them in a way to provide the best possible experience to everyone based on the real-time collective state of the network.

3. **Problems Under AI for India:** (a) In the agriculture domain, ignorance of farmers is resulting in low-yield. If we can build a voice-bot for farmers that can answer their questions about crops/fertilizers/soil etc. over phone this can create a substantial impact. (b) Personalized curriculum and student learning.

6. What Should Budding Data Scientists Do?

I think that the following are the things you need to succeed as a Data Scientist:

1. Having a good understanding of the domain.

2. Math and statistics knowledge.

3. Programming skills beyond the level of just using tools/APIs.

I believe that the shallow API approach many people take towards programming is bad in the long run. Not understanding why and how a model works can never make you a good Data Scientist. Knowing and understanding which tool to use and when is also very important.

In contrast to the "tools based thinking" one needs to think from the fundamental intuition level. It is important to think like a product manager i.e. someone who is building a solution. First, one should formulate a vague business problem into an ML problem e.g. "Optimize the business for Ola Cabs." One needs the ability to convert the problem from this very high level to an ML problem.

I believe that the upcoming Data Scientists should study real business problems, instead of spending all their time on tools like TensorFlow or Spark. I would advise them to go and talk to farmers or doctors. For e.g. they should spend a day in the hospital with nurses/doctors to understand the actual problems and the ground reality.

For e.g. today, in X-rays we have around 30% error rate, which means that chances of misdiagnosis are enormous. In rural areas, a doctor has just one minute for each patient. In such conditions how can humans have high accuracy?

In my view, the real use-cases of Data Science come from sectors such as agriculture, healthcare and education. These are areas where one can make a big impact. Unfortunately, people are not paying enough attention to these.

There are various stages of evolution of a Data Scientist

- **Data Analyst (like car drivers):** API based people who know how to use the model, but don't know what's going on inside.

- **Data Scientist (like a car mechanic):** Knows how to change and make slight tweaks to the algorithm. Knows how the parts work and can change the parts.

- **Researcher (like car designers):** Can come up with new kinds of modelling paradigms.

7. How Should Data Science be Done

Here I present a template for thinking about any AI or Data Science problem

1. **Metrics:** First of all we need to decide on the metrics i.e. what do we want to optimize for. For e.g. at Ola Cab, number of rides fulfilled or utilization of cabs/drivers should be high, cancellation should be low etc. are some important metrics. Define the metrics exactly e.g. CTR/churn etc. Also the definition of the problem and fully understanding the terms involved in it are very important.

2. **Domain Knowledge:** Respect the domain knowledge, what knowledge do you have about the domain? It can help you come up with powerful features for your business problems, especially when you don't have huge data. One has to realize, feature engineering is extremely important

3. **Data Collection:** What stimulus data to collect? It is quite important to decide at what level you want to capture the raw data. You cannot store every bit of data because of obvious limitations. At the same time, you cannot afford to miss any data which contains valuable information impacting the underlying problem statement. Avoiding these two extremes, one has to take a middle ground.

4. **Designing States:** The next step is to convert the stimulus data into states. This is the step that determines what the final model or algorithm will receive as input. States can be simple features or carefully built complex modelled-features. E.g. converting Fitbit's data to health score, or using credit data to compute "discipline," "capacity" and "intention" to pay all of which can be used to compute a final credit score. Another example is in an online education system where, given "logs of students, problems, questions and their score on each question," states could be which concepts does each student understand well and which not so well.

5. **Taking Optimal Actions:** Once we've converted raw data into states, we are ready to take actions based on these states. The action should optimize the chosen metric. There are a variety of ways to compute

the "optimal action" such as (a) optimization of reward function (b) learn through reinforcement learning (c) right action in right state.

6. **Evaluation:** Once the action has been taken we need to evaluate the actions. Any new model needs to be continuously monitored, and has to be evaluated in either offline or online mode through A/B testing and decide whether it's really improving the business objective.

ADDITIONAL THOUGHTS

A Basic Guide to How Data Science Is Done in Industry

Author: Pulkit Bansal

In industry, Data Science is always done with a goal to create a positive business impact. Data scientists are not out there to just build some "cool-stuff". They actually need to work towards meeting a business target for e.g. to increase sales, reduce losses, improve customer retention etc. Also, it's not about how simple or advanced your model is, all that matters in the end is what business impact you have generated. This is a crucial mindset that one needs to acquire, which is to realise that it's not the method or technique that matters, rather it's achieving the goal that is everything.

Knowing about Data Science is one thing, but showing that it actually works is a totally different game. The success of any model is never guaranteed, no matter how much effort has gone into building it or how advanced is the technique. In fact, majority of the models that are developed do not succeed in improving the business. So, one has to make multiple attempts at a problem, and think further each time and analyze what is lacking in the current model, what features are missing, what cases it doesn't handle well etc. to make the model work. Therefore, it is important to be comfortable at handling failure as successful model-building requires a lot of perseverance.

In an industrial setting, a Data Scientist is expected to deliver "maximum value in minimum time." Therefore it is better to first let's say build a model with 80% accuracy in 3 weeks, rather than waiting for 6 months to build an advanced model which has 90% accuracy. This practice is often called "building a first cut model," and is one of the key skills that a Data Scientist must develop. The first-cut model should make intuitive sense, and should try to cover the most important aspects of a problem/data. It doesn't have to be perfect. Rather its something that works decently for the time being. Once this is done, you can proceed to build a more advanced/better model.

The final success of any Data Science team depends crucially on the leader of the team, his decisions and his way of handling things. I think the leader should first of all be a "business-focused" person who is obsessed about creating impact. Secondly, he should have strong quantitative and thinking skills. He doesn't have to be an expert in ML, but he should be able to quickly understand and grasp any ML-algorithm if a need arises. He should most importantly possess extremely good judgement of what idea/algorithm makes sense and what does not.

A leader should expect a solution idea and implementation-plan from the Data Scientists in his team, and should not be satisfied unless the proposed solution is of high quality. But, only he should give the final approval on whether the solution should be implemented, as well as take credit for the success of the solution. Although if there are mistakes in engineering/implementation of the solution, then it's the responsibility of the Data Scientist. In my opinion, if a leader likes to get too deeply involved in engineering at the expense of thinking/making-decisions about the solutions, then he is not a good fit.

Finally, I think that businesses also need to think properly about how to get the most out of their Data Scientists. Firstly, they need to educate their Data Scientists more about their business. Also, the incentives should be designed properly so that a Data Scientist feels motivated and driven towards generating business-value, and do so fast. Incorrect handling of Data Scientists can make them feel lost, and they may end up building "black-boxes" which are of no use for anybody. The Data Scientists should be backed-up and given freedom to do more experiments, and should also be encouraged to come up with ideas that can improve the business.

How Can a Data Scientist Become Better at Engineering?

Author: Pulkit Bansal

Here, I refer engineering as "all the tech-work a Data Scientist needs to do to make his solution work in practice." The focus of this essay will be only on the kind of engineering relevant for a Data Scientist.

The most fundamental engineering skill is having an ability to convert any idea or an algorithm in mind into a working code in a programming language such as Python/R/C++. The best way to acquire this skill is practice; one should practice solving a lot of algorithmic problems from competitive-programming portals. For a given problem, you can look at the algorithm in detail, but you should try to code it up yourself without looking at the solution. You can start with simple problems, and slowly work your way up to more difficult ones. I would also highly recommend doing a proper course on algorithms and data-structures, to train your mind to think algorithmically.

During implementation of any solution, though it is useful to follow a list of "best engineering practices," it is even more important to think about "what properties my solution should have?" and anticipate "where can things go wrong?." Some examples could be:

- How much will my model get affected if last two days data don't get logged in the database? Would my model fail or produce bad output?

- What if the model training step fails today? Do I have a backup plan?

- Is it easy to make small changes to my code. For e.g. if I want to add another feature to the machine learning model will I need to re-write the whole code?

- How do I reduce unexpected behaviour from the model? If it happens, how do I get notified about this? What sanity checks should I put in place?

Therefore, before starting any coding, one should first properly think and plan how the implementation will be done. Unfortunately "proper-thinking" is a highly ignored skill, especially in this era where there is over-emphasis on being "hands-on." But, truly good engineers whom I've worked with, put significant time and effort in thinking, and the result is a bug-free code which many others can reuse, and which lasts for years to come. In summary "better thinking" is a crucial aspect, which ultimately leads to "better engineering."

Finally, I want to say that though one should not try to achieve mastery of a hundred different tools, but it is very important to develop an "engineering-attitude." This means having a strong inclination towards not just designing a solution, but actually implementing it and making it work. One should be ready to learn any new tool, or break through any technical hurdle in the way of successfully deploying the model.

Does Advanced Mathematics Have Any Relevance in Data Science?

Author: Pulkit Bansal

These days a lot of people are saying that one can easily do "applied Data Science" without knowing much mathematics. I agree with this statement to the extent that you wouldn't be writing much of proofs and equations, or using calculus in your daily work. But still I would argue that, to be an effective Data Scientist one has to be comfortable with mathematical/algorithmic reasoning. Let me start by giving some examples of questions that Data Scientists deal with on a day to day basis:

- Should I build a separate model for each city, or a single model for all the cities?

- What is the right metric for this problem: "finding the most influential people in human history based on Wikipedia data"?

- Why is my gradient-boosting model unable to beat a basic rule-based model?

- I have installed a library that implements a recommendation-model which optimizes for showing most relevant items to a user. How do I tweak it so that it maximizes my revenue instead?

All these questions require critical thinking & reasoning ability, and mathematical understanding. One good way to develop this ability is to actively study quantitative/algorithmic subjects during your college degree or afterwards. These subjects don't necessarily have to be taken from math courses; they could also belong to diverse areas such as signals-and-systems, computational biology, randomized-algorithms or econometrics etc. The subject-area is not important, as long as the course engages the quantitative side of your mind.

Till a decade back, most of the "Data Science" being done in industrial-setup (except for some industries like Finance) was actually based on arithmetic and elementary statistics like mean/median/variance. In fact, doing a weighted-average or linear-regression was considered as advanced-modelling back then. Now the requirements have increased, and if you want to really understand current ML algorithms, you can't do without knowing the basics of calculus, linear algebra as well as probability theory.

But, I will suggest people to also study some advanced mathematic courses e.g. measure theory, differential geometry or functional analysis. Although presently such knowledge has rare direct application, as the world shifts towards even more ambitious problems such as "artificial general intelligence," I strongly believe that we'll see advanced math being increasingly applied. In fact, stochastic calculus has been extensively used in the field of quantitative finance since the 1970s.

Another motivation to study more advanced mathematics is to strengthen your mental ability, which makes it easier to grasp fundamental ML concepts. Even though the mathematics of current ML seems elementary, one has to put significant effort to properly understand things such as "how and why backpropagation works?," "Why do we use cross-entropy error?," "Why do LSTM equations make sense?." But if you've levelled up your brain, these things will become less daunting.

Finally, I think that it's hard to enjoy your work if you don't understand what you are doing. If you'll keep doing things with a black box approach, at some point you might just get bored with your work. In contrast when you really understand what you do, why you do, and how you do, it makes the work more exciting, and you're more motivated, which is definitely something we all ultimately seek.

Some "Thumb Rules" for Working Better as a Data Scientist

Author: Pulkit Bansal

I want to share some simple rules I've learnt from my experience in my career in Data Science. I wish I knew them earlier

1. **Employ Simplicity More Often:** Sometimes the problems are extremely complex for e.g. optimizing for multiple objectives and constraints. In such cases defining the problem precisely can itself become a challenge. For such situations, one should simplify the problem definition or limit its scope so that the problem becomes more approachable, without losing its broad meaning. Even with solutions, one should not be afraid to first design something simple and experiment with it. Then by analyzing where the simple solution doesn't work, one can gain insights and more effectively improve it. Often 60–80% of the problem can be solved by just using a good simple solution. One should not mistake "simple" for "lacking in thought," because what "simple" actually means is that you're still putting your full thought on the problem but only focusing on its essential aspects, and you want your solution to get implemented quickly. Even though you want to build a not-so-complicated solution, you still want to make it as effective as possible.

2. **Don't Get Lost in the Details:** Our work involves analyzing huge amounts of information (big-data). In such an environment it is easy to lose sight of the big picture and one may spend too much time caring about inconsequential matters. Being detail-oriented is a virtue in our trade, but since time is precious we must spend most of it on analyzing the most essential things. We often deal with

tables containing 100s of fields, but the essence of it is contained in just a handful of columns. This again relates to the "simplicity" point above.

3. **Work on Problems with High Upside:** If your goal is to create impact, the best chance is typically when you're working on a new problem. If a problem has a good existing solution, improving it further is always a challenge. Also, one learns more when building a new solution from scratch, rather than doing just incremental work. In my opinion, a business-focused Data Scientist should choose the problem while keeping the potential for impact in mind.

4. **Spend More Time Thinking:** In my opinion, the success of any ML project depend on: (1) Problem formulation and domain knowledge (25%) (2) Thinking and proper solution design (60%) (3) Engineering (15%). Unfortunately, Data Scientists often spend the least amount of time on the most important part which is "thinking about the solution," and disproportionately large amount of time on engineering. I guess it's because engineering keeps you busy, and you feel like you're "doing something," whereas thinking can be hard and frustrating as you may not make major progress even after a few hours of thinking. But I cannot overstate the importance of thinking, because the decisions about what approach/algorithm you'll take to solve a problem is the chief-determinant of whether a project will succeed. Implementation and proper engineering can take months of effort, and if the decision is wrong then that entire effort can go wasted. Therefore, I would always err on the side of spending a few extra days in the design of the solution, discuss it with a few people, get more opinion, and select only the best approach keeping all pros and cons in mind before beginning the implementation.

About the Authors

Pulkit currently works as a Lead Data Scientist at MakeMyTrip in Bangalore. Previously he has worked at Adobe, and before that he worked in Quant roles at WorldQuant and Goldman Sachs. He is a graduate from IIT Kanpur with dual degree in Mathematics and Scientific Computing. Outside work, he enjoys reading about history and likes to engage in physical activities such as Trekking, workout.

Kunal currently works as Research Scientist at InMobi Bangalore. He has worked on large scale Recommendation Systems and transaction prediction for ad bidders. He graduated from IIT Kharagpur with a B.Tech. degree in Electronics and Electrical Communcation Engg. He loves to read about and watch movies across languages and is ready to go out for good food any day any time. :)

Pankaj is currently working as a Senior Data Scientist at ShareChat, and is a graduate from IIT Kanpur with dual degree in Mathematics and Scientific Computing. He is machine learning enthusiast with particular interests in deep learning. His favorite pastimes involve running, trekking and travelling. He loves to read and learn about new technologies.

Srijan currently works as a Senior Data Scientist at ShareChat. He has worked on recommendation problems and has been involved in developing the content processing pipeline which is the backbone of ShareChat. Before joining ShareChat, he was working as a Data Scientist at Fidelity Investments, Bangalore. He worked there on NLP problems and used it to develop recommendation systems & build predictive models.

Neeraj currently works as an Analyst at Goldman Sachs. He has done summer internship with Worldquant and also has worked as part time research consultant with them for about a year.